# PASTA

# PASTA

## RECIPES FROM THE KITCHEN OF
## THE AMERICAN ACADEMY IN ROME

---

BY CHRISTOPHER BOSWELL

WITH ELENA GOLDBLATT

---

PHOTOGRAPHY BY ANNIE SCHLECHTER

ROME
SUSTAINABLE
FOOD
PROJECT

The Little Bookroom

New York

© 2013 The Little Bookroom
Text and recipes © 2013 Christopher Boswell
Photographs © 2013 Annie Schlechter, except as noted below
Photo pages 77 and 148 courtesy of The Rome Sustainable Food Project
Book design: Annie Schlechter
Book production: Adam Hess

Library of Congress Cataloging-in-Publication Data

Boswell, Christopher.
Pasta : recipes from the kitchen of the American Academy in Rome /
by Christopher Boswell with Elena Goldblatt ;
photography by Annie Schlechter.
pages cm
Includes bibliographical references and index.
ISBN 978-1-936941-02-5 (hardback)
1. Cooking (Pasta)  2. Cooking, Italian.  I. Goldblatt, Elena.
II. American Academy in Rome. III. Title.
TX809.M17B67 2013
641.82'2—dc23
2013009847

Printed in The United States of America

Published by The Little Bookroom
435 Hudson Street, Suite 3000
New York NY 10014
editorial@littlebookroom.com
www.littlebookroom.com

ISBN 978-1-936941-02-5

10 9 8 7 6 5 4 3 2 1

# TABLE OF CONTENTS

# FOREWORD

Every morning, as our pastry cook, Mirella Missenti, writes the daily menu on the blackboard at the bar of the American Academy, Fellows clamor around to see what's for lunch. Of course, in Italy, pasta is the centerpiece of the meal, and we design our menus around the pasta dish we've chosen for that day. Come lunchtime, we hurry the piping hot pasta to the buffet. It is usually the last thing to go out because, as Italians like to say, *la pasta non aspetta nessuno* ("the pasta waits for no one").

Since its inception in February 2007, the Rome Sustainable Food Project has been a teaching kitchen in which interns learn the basics of Italian and seasonal cooking. Teaching how to make a great *piatto di pasta* is essential, and making fresh pasta is a milestone moment for many interns.

Italian culinary traditions are incredibly important to us here at the RSFP. Our philosophy and teaching model is based on fostering these traditions and preserving them for posterity. All of the recipes in this book are built on these traditions. Over the years we've added a twist of our own from our experience at Chez Panisse and cooking seasonal and traditional Roman food.

In this book, recipes and sections function like building blocks. The fundamental techniques of one type of pasta or sauce will give you the tools to approach the next one. The layout of the book reflects the way in which we teach the interns. They start by making simple pasta dishes and progressively acquire the skills to make more complex ones. The book is also profoundly based on the seasonal cycle of produce. Finally, *Pasta* is a book about the community at the American Academy and the special moments and memories that mark the time spent on the Janiculum Hill in Rome.

*In bocca al lupo e buon appetito!*

Christopher Boswell
Rome

# PASTA IN THE RSFP KITCHEN

*Saranno i maccheroni, vi giuro, che uniranno l'Italia.*
*It will be maccheroni, I swear to you, that will unite Italy.*
—Giuseppe Garibaldi, upon liberating Naples in 1860

Pasta is the national food of Italy, yet despite Garibaldi's claims, it is by no means a unifying dish. From north to south and east to west it seems that each town has its unique and incontestable pasta shape and way of preparing a *piatto di pasta* that is fixed in time and rooted in tradition. I am always awed by the depth and diversity of Italian cuisine. In fact, one of the beautiful and remarkable things about Italy is that in this land of deep traditions, there are endless paradoxes and exceptions ingrained in local customs. Each dish tells the story of a place, its history, its people, its climate, and its way of life.

While the origins of pasta may be more than 1,200 years old, the invention in the early 1800s of machines that could make and dry pasta en masse revolutionized the way Italians ate. Pasta as an everyday food became prevalent first in southern Italy and then in the north. Until then, pasta was reserved for very special occasions and for the very wealthy. By the 1940s pasta had become a truly popular dish, and I mean popular in the literal sense of the word. Pasta became something every Italian—rich or poor, urban or rural—ate in thousands of shapes and sizes.

At its heart pasta is simple and unpretentious. But it is also complex and idiosyncratic. I'm always amazed that something so simple made of flour and water or egg can be so incredibly diverse and endlessly creative. Pasta can be found both in its dried form (pasta *secca*) and in its fresh form (pasta *fresca*). Don't think of dry pasta as the dried version of fresh pasta—they are entirely different.

Dry pasta is the most common form of pasta, sold worldwide, with a long shelf life. It is never very expensive, but the difference in quality can be astounding. Quality is almost always correlated with price and paying a little more is always worth it. (Instead of thinking about why something is relatively expensive, think of what it means for a product that is labor intensive and so specific to be relatively inexpensive.) The best pasta, of course, is that made in Italy with Italian durum wheat flour and extruded through bronze dies.

Fresh pasta is less common and quite special because it is labor intensive. Fresh pasta is usually synonymous with egg pasta, but there are amazing flour and water types from Southern Italy that are less known. Fresh pasta is usually made with soft-wheat flour and water, vegetable puree, or eggs. Filled pasta and lasagna are almost always made with egg pasta. You can also find "dry" egg pasta if you're in a pinch, but I would recommend making or buying fresh pasta (at *pastifici* or specialty shops), whenever possible, for the most flavor and the best texture.

In Italy, pasta is served in three distinct ways: pasta *asciutta*, pasta *in brodo*, and pasta *al forno*. *Pasta asciutta* is the most common way Italians eat pasta. It is called *asciutta*, or "dry," because it is simply tossed with sauce and not served in broth. Somewhat ironically, both fresh and dry pasta can fall under the umbrella of *pasta asciutta* when they are served with sauce. Conversely, *pasta in brodo* is "wet," because it is served in broth. Lastly, *pasta al forno* is boiled first and then baked in the oven with sauce and cheese. We teach the interns at the RSFP to think of pasta according to these three categories.

Whether fresh or dry, *asciutta, in brodo,* or *al forno*, it all starts the same way: pasta always relies on some form of fat for flavor (such as olive oil, butter, or lard) and *nearly* every recipe is served with cheese to complement the ingredients in the dish. These two major ingredients are constants—staples if you will—in the following recipes. Other important ingredients, such as fish, pork, and ricotta, play significant supporting roles in our kitchen. Like fat and cheese, they merit detailed discussion, and bits of information about them are scattered throughout the book.

In addition, pasta shapes and pasta sauces are inextricably linked. Nowadays, we perceive these as almost natural and instinctive pairings that are ingrained in the way Italians think about pasta. Yet what we now consider canonical pairings aren't all that obvious; they stem from centuries of pasta-making traditions with profound historical, regional, seasonal, and liturgical roots.

Each dish in this book tells a story. It pairs a pasta shape with a specific sauce based on these traditions, but also on our years of experience at the Rome Sustainable Food Project and at Chez Panisse, where we aim for exceptional and balanced dishes in which the pasta and sauce are perfectly complementary both in texture and in taste. In short: all the above factors—the history, the ingredients, the imagination and creativity of countless generations—ensure that the story told on the plate is one of tradition, flavor, sustainability, and profound respect for each ingredient.

One final practical note: In Italy, *un pacco di pasta* (500 g) serves four people, but somehow it always seems to serve more in the United States. These recipes for dry pasta are designed for 1 lb (or 454 g) of pasta and the recipes for fresh pasta are designed for about 1.3 lbs (600 g) of pasta. All the recipes in the book serve four to six hungry people. If pasta is the first course and not the main dish, these recipes can serve up to eight people.

## GRASSO · *Fat*

Italy is a land of inflexible food rules and deeply rooted traditions. Nowadays, we often think of Italy as a land divided between north and south. This divide holds true when it comes to most food things, and it is especially true when it comes to the kind of fat Italians use in their cooking. There is a "fat line" that starts in Tuscany: butter is predominantly used north of the Tuscan border (with the exception of Liguria because of its Mediterranean climate), and olive oil is primarily used in the south.

Yet this dichotomy represents a very modern understanding of how the cuisines of northern and southern Italy differ. This divergence is just over 150 years old, dating back to the Unification of Italy in 1861. Only when we talk of Italy as a united country can we consider a north-south divide. For centuries the divide was socioeconomic, not geographical, separating the very wealthy who could afford luxurious butter and olive oil from everyone else. All Italians primarily used animal fat in the form of lard for cooking, as it was the cheapest and most easily accessible form of fat. Nothing was thrown out when a pig was butchered.

Italy has undergone enormous socio-economic change in the last century that has deeply affected its cuisine. As Italy became richer and industrialized, many traditional recipes evolved to incorporate "lighter" fat. Olive oil or butter was substituted for lard and our modern conception of Italian cuisine was created. Northerners indulged in butter, as the green pastures of the North are perfect to raise dairy cows. Southerners extolled the benefits of olive oil, since the hot sunny summers and mild winters of the Mediterranean are ideal for olive groves to thrive.

At the RSFP we are committed to following these culinary traditions, thus telling the story of each dish. We always use butter for preparing the regional dishes of northern Italy. Most of our recipes hail from central and southern Italy, however, and call for olive oil. We exclusively use extra virgin olive oil. For everyday cooking we like to use oil from Sabina in Northern Lazio, since, even in Roman times, it was prized for its versatility because of its low acidity.

## FORMAGGIO · *Cheese*

Almost every pasta at the RSFP is served with freshly grated cheese. These cheeses play an essential supporting role in many dishes. Grana Padano and Parmigiano-Reggiano are both types of Grana, characteristically grainy, hard, and mature cow's milk cheeses from northern Italy. Parmigiano-Reggiano and Grana Padano are D.O.P. products (the denomination of origin is protected). Parmigiano can only be called "Parmigiano-Reggiano" if it abides to a stringent set of rules and is produced in specific provinces, while Grana Padano can be made over a much wider area in the Pianura Padana. Parmigiano-Reggiano is aged for at least two years, while

Grana Padano is aged for a minimum of nine months. Parmigiano-Reggiano has been produced in the same way since the Middle Ages and Grana Padano for even longer—its origins and techniques could be more than 1,000 years old.

Pecorino Romano is probably the oldest cheese of them all. It has been produced in virtually the same manner for more than 2,000 years. Pecorino Romano is also a D.O.P. product made from the milk of sheep raised in Lazio, southern Tuscany, and some parts of Sardinia. It needs to be aged for a minimum of eight months. Pecorino Romano is a crucial component of Roman, central, and southern cooking, and is praised for its distinct and powerful sharp flavor.

At the RSFP we almost always serve pasta with freshly grated Grana Padano. In my opinion, the younger Grana has a milder, more delicate perfume and subtle sharpness than Parmigiano-Reggiano. Grana is better suited to the RSFP style of cooking, allowing for more clean, subtle, and balanced pairings. There are of course some exceptions: Parmigiano-Reggiano is the best accompaniment to the robust food of Emilia-Romagna (where the cheese originated) because its acidity and sharpness help cut through the dairy-rich cuisine.

All our Roman, central, and southern dishes that call for cheese are usually served with freshly grated Pecorino Romano. We also like to serve some of them with shavings of freshly grated Ricotta Salata, which provides a wonderful creamy saltiness that rounds out the flavors of many dishes.

The taste of cheese quickly deteriorates once it is grated. Buy chunks of cheese and grate it yourself right before you need it using the small holes in a box grater or a microplane.

## PASTA FUNDAMENTALS

### THE POT & THE LID

A large (7-quart/7-liter) stockpot with a heavy bottom is ideal as it allows for even and consistent heat distribution. We suggest using a non-reactive pot such as a stainless steel one.

Put the pot of water over high heat to bring it to a boil. You can use a lid to accelerate the boiling process, but do not cover the pot once you've dropped the pasta. The water should be at a constant simmer as the pasta cooks; using a lid would cause the water to boil rapidly and aggressively, which risks breaking the pasta. Furthermore, pasta releases starch that makes water foamy, and covering the pot with a lid could cause it to boil over.

### THE COLANDER

Some pots come with a colander insert, which is ideal because it allows you to quickly transfer the pasta along with some cooking water. A colander or strainer in the sink is perfectly fine—just make sure to reserve some cooking water before you strain the pasta.

## THE WOODEN SPOON

Use a wooden spoon with soft edges for cooking pasta and for making sauce. A metal spoon can cut the pasta and scratch the pan.

## THE COOKING WATER

Cook the pasta in lots of water, about 2 gallons (7.5 l) for 1 lb (454 g) of pasta. Pasta absorbs a large amount of water as it cooks and needs to be submerged at all times.

## THE SALT

Italians always use coarse sea salt to season cooking water, and we do the same at the RSFP. If you can't find it, finely ground sea salt is more readily available and is an acceptable substitution. Salt the water only after it has come to a rolling boil. Salt is a corrosive and the pot could pit if you add it to cold water (since metal expands as it heats up).

Use 2 ounces (about 3 tablespoons) of coarse sea salt for 2 gallons of water.

If your cooking water is under-seasoned, the dish will always seem under-salted regardless of how the sauce is seasoned.

## AL DENTE

The amount of time the pasta cooks is crucial. Timing is everything. Pasta must be served when it is perfectly al dente, which literally means "to the tooth" and describes the moment when pasta is cooked to the ideal point of tenderness. The inner core stays bone white and retains a pleasant bite.

# PASTA SECCA

# PASTA SECCA
## DRY PASTA

There are hundreds if not thousands of types of dry pasta, ranging from the ultrafamous spaghetti to the more obscure strozzapreti. Each pasta has unique properties that make it pair wonderfully with specific sauces. Below are the dry pasta shapes used in this book. Think of these as types of shapes that have a similar function, for example spaghetti and linguine are both a kind of long rather thick pasta. If you can't find one specific type try to use a pasta type that is similar in shape so that it is balanced with the sauce it has been paired within the recipe.

This page: left column top to bottom: Farfalle, Fusilli, Gnocchetti Sardi, Orecchiette. Right column: top to bottom: Conchiglie, Strozzapreti, Trofie, Ruote. Center bottom: Pizzichi di Farro. Opposite page: left column top to bottom: Garganelli, Penne, Rigatoni/Tortiglioni, Paccheri, Calamarata, Mezze Maniche, Ditalini. Right column left to right: Bucatini, Spaghetti, Linguine/Bavette.

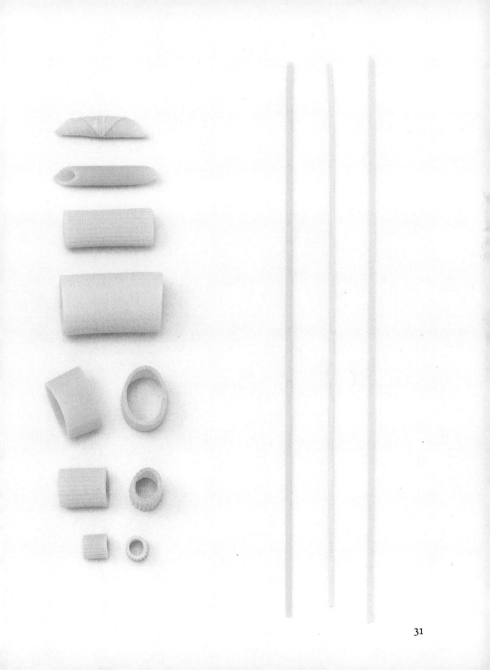

# OLIO

## OIL-BASED SAUCES

In the RSFP kitchen, interns are first taught how to make oil-based pasta sauces. The techniques of *olio* sauces are extremely important since they serve as a foundation for virtually all other pasta dishes.

The principal technique is the skillful execution of a *soffritto*. The *soffritto* is the base of the sauce. It is a mix of garlic, aromatic vegetables, herbs and spices (almost always including hot pepper flakes); maybe even a little meat. The *soffritto* is gently fried in olive oil, butter, or lard over medium-low heat. The ingredients in the *soffritto* serve as supportive flavors that enhance the aroma of the main ingredients of the dish.

The simplicity of a *soffritto* can be illusive, because this kind of simplicity leaves very little room for error. In the most basic pasta recipe, Aglio, Olio e Peperoncino, the *soffritto* actually *is* the sauce. Incredibly simple and delicious when made correctly, if even one of these ingredients is off in the slightest way, shape, or form, the dish will be either completely lackluster or noticeably out of balance.

Cooking the *soffritto* over medium-low heat for a few minutes—as opposed to cooking it over high heat for a few seconds—allows for the essential oils found in two of the most commonly used ingredients in the *soffritto*, garlic and hot pepper, to bind with the olive oil over time (since fat bonds with fat), creating a garlicky and spicy oil infusion. If the heat is too high, you risk burning the ingredients, which adds a bitter flavor. Do not rush making your *soffritto*: slow cooking over a low flame creates a more pronounced infusion that makes the dish exceptional. The principles of a *soffritto* always remain the same.

Oil-based sauces are tossed with pasta cooked perfectly al dente. Working quickly is important here. The pasta should be drained well and immediately transferred to the pan or bowl and tossed quickly so that the oil condiment can fully adhere to the pasta.

# SPAGHETTI AGLIO, OLIO E PEPERONCINO
## SPAGHETTI WITH OLIVE OIL, GARLIC
## & HOT PEPPER FLAKES

_____

*The American Academy is the home away from home for the community of artists and scholars who work and reside here over the course of the academic year. We love to prepare this dish in the fall when we harvest fresh peperoncini from the Bass Garden, and the Fellows first arrive in Rome. This is the classic southern Italian go-to dish when no one in the family can agree on what they want to eat—everybody loves Aglio, Olio e Peperoncino. Who knew something so simple could be so good? Only five of the most basic ingredients are needed for this sauce; you probably won't even need to shop for them. Traditionally this pasta is eaten without cheese, but the addition of breadcrumbs is widely accepted because it doesn't interfere with the simplicity of the flavors and adds great texture. Make sure the garlic doesn't turn brown. Browning the garlic too much produces a pronounced bitter flavor in the oil that you will be able to taste (and smell) from a mile away.*

⅓ cup (79 ml) extra virgin olive oil

4 garlic cloves, smashed

1½ teaspoons hot pepper flakes

15 parsley sprigs, picked and chopped (about 4 tablespoons)

1 lb (454 g) spaghetti

1 cup toasted breadcrumbs (see p. 237)

Bring a large pot of cold water to a boil.

Put the olive oil and garlic in a 14-inch (36-cm) sauté pan over medium-low heat. Fry the garlic very slowly in the olive oil until it is light golden all over. If it seems to be gaining color too fast, turn the heat to low.

Add the hot pepper and parsley immediately, let sizzle for 15 seconds, turn off the heat, and set the pan aside. Immediately add about a ¼ cup (60 ml) cooking water to the pan to halt the frying of the garlic, parsley, and hot pepper.

Drop the spaghetti into boiling salted water and cook, stirring frequently, until the pasta is al dente. Drain it, reserving ¼ cup (60 ml) cooking water. Transfer the spaghetti to the pan right away and toss well to combine, adding cooking water as necessary. Top with breadcrumbs and serve.

# RIGATONI ALLA GRICIA
## RIGATONI WITH GUANCIALE, PECORINO & BLACK PEPPER

———

*Pasta alla Gricia is one of the Roman classics, a real must-have for one's repertoire, and it's incredibly easy to make. The key to making this simple pasta really shine is the quality of the ingredients and how you use them. Make sure you grind the pepper at the last minute and use real pecorino Romano. If the guanciale doesn't have pepper on it, make sure to add lots of freshly ground black pepper at the end. Get the guanciale (or artisanally produced bacon, if you can't find guanciale) nice and crispy—it makes a world of difference, trust me.*

*2 tablespoons extra virgin olive oil*

*8 oz (227 g) guanciale, pancetta, or artisanal bacon, cut into ½-inch (1.2-cm) dice*

*3 garlic cloves, smashed*

*1 teaspoon hot pepper flakes*

*1 lb (454 g) rigatoni*

*3 oz (85 g) pecorino Romano, grated (about ¾ cup)*

*Freshly ground black pepper, to taste*

Bring a large pot of cold water to a boil.

Put the olive oil and guanciale in a 14-inch (36-cm) sauté pan over medium-low heat.

Once the guanciale has started to render its fat and brown, add the garlic and turn the heat to low.

When the garlic is golden, add the hot pepper. Let sizzle for 30 seconds and immediately add a small spoonful of cooking water to prevent the ingredients from burning. If the guanciale isn't quite crispy enough yet, remove the garlic so that it doesn't burn and keep cooking over low heat until the guanciale is nice and crispy, then turn off the heat.

Drop the rigatoni in boiling salted water and cook, stirring frequently, until the pasta is al dente. Drain it, reserving ¼ cup (60 ml) cooking water. Transfer the rigatoni to the pan right away, add 2 tablespoons pecorino and toss well to coat the rigatoni with the guanciale fat, adding cooking water as necessary.

Top with copious amounts of freshly grated pecorino and pepper, and serve immediately.

# PESCE

## SUSTAINABLE FISH

We are facing an unprecedented global fishing crisis with devastating repercussions on the environment, our health, and the global economy. Our current fishing practices and consumption habits are such that many species that once seemed innumerable are in imminent danger of extinction. This crisis is particularly acute in the Mediterranean. Experts estimate that more than forty species in the Mediterranean alone are in great danger of extinction due to overfishing and unsustainable fishing practices.

Farming fish, at first thought to be a viable solution to the depletion of wild fish populations, unfortunately also raises many concerns. Farmed fish often live in very cramped spaces and are usually fed potentially harmful antibiotics and other chemicals in order to keep them "healthy." In addition, the pens used can cause pollution and alter local eco-systems.

Defining and identifying sustainable practices for seafood (wild or farm-raised) can be rather tricky. It's difficult to trace wild fish populations to know what waters they have traveled in, what they have eaten, and what toxins or pollution they may have encountered in their lifetimes. Greenpeace defines seafood as sustainable if it "comes from a fishery with practices that can be maintained indefinitely without reducing the target species' ability to maintain its population and without adversely impacting on other species within the ecosystem by removing their food source, accidentally killing them, or damaging their physical environment."

At the RSFP we rarely use fish, but when we do, we choose the most sustainable seafood native to the Mediterranean Sea just a few miles away from Rome. We buy only local small bluefish, squid, and bivalves, since they don't absorb as many toxins as larger fish because they are smaller in size, reproduce at an earlier age, and have a shorter life span.

# SPAGHETTI ALLE VONGOLE
## SPAGHETTI WITH CLAMS, GARLIC & HOT PEPPER

When Mona Talbott and I were starting the Rome Sustainable Food Project, we wanted to find a local fisherman who practiced sustainable fishing. It turned out that Romano, a man who had worked at the Academy for many years, was a real foodie. One day, he agreed to accompany me to Fiumicino where the Tiber River meets the Mediterranean. The next week we found a fisherman who would sell sustainable fresh fish to the Academy. With the clams we bought from him, Romano taught me how to make Spaghetti alle Vongole the way his wife used to make it. He said her secret was the one or two spoonfuls of tomato liquid that she added. The tomato shouldn't be enough to taste or to see, but should be enough to neutralize the salinity of the clams and help the pasta cling to the sauce. Most important, it should be that "secret ingredient" that people can't quite put their finger on, but that makes the dish.

⅓ cup (79 ml) extra virgin olive oil

3 garlic cloves, smashed

2 lbs (907 g) Manila, littleneck, or razor clams, or a combination of the three, rinsed under running water for 30 minutes

1 cup (237 ml) dry white wine, preferably from the Castelli Romani

1 to 2 tablespoons tomato juice, from canned tomatoes

1 lb (454 g) spaghetti

1 teaspoon hot pepper flakes

15 parsley sprigs, picked and chopped (about 4 tablespoons)

Bring a large pot of cold water to a boil.

Put the olive oil and garlic in a 14-inch (36-cm) sauté pan over medium heat. Gently fry the garlic, stirring occasionally, until it is just golden, then remove and discard it.

Add the clams to the pan, turn the heat to medium-high and let them sear for 1 minute, stirring so that the clams form an even layer across the bottom of the pan; there should be an intense hushing and searing sound.

Add the white wine and tomato juice and quickly cover the pan with a lid to help steam open the clams. After about 2 minutes remove the lid. The shells should be opening.

Drop the spaghetti into boiling lightly salted water (salt the water very lightly, as the clams will release salt into the sauce making it very salty, which will be fine as long as the cooking water isn't overly salty). Cook the spaghetti, stirring frequently, until the pasta is almost al dente.

Meanwhile, when the clams have opened, remove them from the pan and place them in a bowl. Discard any clams that have not opened.

Let the remaining clam juice cook down until it has reduced by half, then add the hot pepper and the parsley and turn off the heat.

Drain the spaghetti 3 minutes before the indicated cooking time, reserving ¾ cup (237 ml) cooking water. The pasta will cook for the last few minutes in the sauce and absorb its flavors.

Transfer the spaghetti to the sauté pan and turn the heat to medium-high. Simmer the pasta in the sauce, adding cooking water as necessary and stirring frequently to avoid sticking. Top with clams.

# SPAGHETTI COZZE, PACHINO E PECORINO
## SPAGHETTI WITH MUSSELS, CHERRY TOMATOES & PECORINO

*Pasta all'Amatriciana is a classic Roman dish made with guanciale, tomato sauce, and pecorino Romano. Some people know it as l'Amatriciana del Mare, the Amatriciana of the sea, because in this recipe the mussels take the place of the guanciale and the cherry tomatoes take the place of the tomato sauce to create a light summer dish. Although it originated along the southern coast of Italy and in Puglia, this dish has become a Roman staple in many trattorie.*

*In Italy it is usually considered a cardinal sin to add cheese to any fish dish, but this is one of those rare (and delicious) exceptions. The salty briny mussels work well with a salty sheep's milk cheese. Mussels' meaty flesh have a very bold flavor that can stand up to pecorino; their slight brininess is fantastic when paired with sweet cherry tomatoes, and the pecorino really ties it all together. Don't substitute clams for mussels—clams have a far more delicate sea flavor, also briny, but in a very different way. Pecorino and tomatoes complement the vibrant mussels, but overpower the more subtle flavor of clams.*

⅓ cup (79 ml) extra virgin olive oil

3 garlic cloves, smashed

2 lbs (907 g) black mussels, scrubbed clean and debearded

½ cup (118 ml) dry white wine, preferably a Frascati from the Castelli Romani

1 lb (454 g) cherry tomatoes, cut in half

1 teaspoon hot pepper flakes

20 parsley sprigs, picked and chopped (about 6 tablespoons)

1 lb (454 g) spaghetti

2 oz (57 g) pecorino Romano, grated (about ½ cup)

Bring a large pot of cold water to a boil.

Put the olive oil and garlic in a 14-inch (36-cm) sauté pan over low heat. Gently cook the garlic, stirring occasionally, until it is just golden, then remove and discard it. Immediately add the mussels and raise the heat to high. When you start to hear a sizzling sound, after about 30 seconds, add the white wine.

Quickly cover the pan to help steam the mussels open. After about 3 or 4 minutes remove the lid and let the mussels simmer until their shells have opened and they have released their juices. Remove the open mussels from the pan and place them in a bowl. Discard any mussels that have not opened.

Let the mussel juice in the pan cook down until it has reduced by half. Add the cherry tomatoes, hot pepper, and parsley, and turn the heat off. Taste and adjust the seasoning.

Drop the spaghetti into boiling salted water and cook, stirring frequently, until the pasta is almost al dente. Drain the spaghetti 2 minutes before the indicated cooking time, reserving ½ cup (118 ml) cooking water. The pasta will cook for the last few minutes in the sauce and absorb its flavors.

Transfer the spaghetti to the pan and turn the heat to medium-high. Simmer the pasta in the sauce for about 2 minutes, adding cooking water as necessary and stirring frequently to avoid sticking. Top with the mussels, then sprinkle abundantly with pecorino and serve immediately.

# LINGUINE ALLA PUTTANESCA IN BIANCO
## LINGUINE WITH "WHITE" PUTTANESCA SAUCE

---

*Elena Goldblatt was an intern at the RSFP in the fall of 2011. One day in November, our sous chef Giovanni Guerrera needed a pasta dish for the menu, and, since we had no tomatoes, Elena suggested making a puttanesca in bianco. In November, when fresh tomatoes can no longer be found and we are waiting to receive our D.O.P. canned tomatoes, we have to live without tomatoes for a few weeks, which isn't always easy. This pasta came as a pleasant surprise. I love the big bold salty flavors of pasta alla puttanesca, and the flavors are beautifully complemented, in this interpretation, by the spicy garlicky oil, the sweet onions, and the crunchy breadcrumbs. A delicious variation can be made with the addition of hook-and-line-caught tuna, which has been poached in olive oil, and fresh marjoram.*

¼ cup (60 ml) extra virgin olive oil, plus 3 tablespoons

1 medium red onion, thinly sliced

3 tablespoons salt-packed capers, rinsed and chopped (see p. 244)

½ cup Gaeta or oil-cured olives, pitted and chopped

3 garlic cloves, chopped

2 teaspoons hot pepper flakes

8 anchovy filets or 4 salt-cured anchovies, cleaned (see p. 244)

¼ teaspoon dried oregano

20 parsley sprigs, picked and chopped (about 6 tablespoons)

1 lb (454 g) linguine

1 cup toasted breadcrumbs (see p. 237)

Bring a large pot of cold water to a boil.

Put 3 tablespoons olive oil, onions, and a pinch of salt in a 14-inch (36-cm) sauté pan over medium heat and cook, stirring occasionally, until the onions are translucent.

Make a well in the onions and add the remaining olive oil. When the oil is hot, add the capers, olives, garlic, and hot pepper and fry, stirring occasionally, until the capers are crispy. Add the anchovies along with the oregano and half of the parsley and sizzle until the anchovies are broken up and have melted into the oil. Turn off the heat and add about ¼ cup (60 ml) cooking water to the pan to halt the frying.

Drop the linguine into boiling salted water and cook, stirring frequently, until the pasta is al dente. Drain it, reserving ¼ cup (60 ml) cooking water. Transfer the linguine to the sauté pan with the remaining parsley and toss well to combine, adding cooking water only as necessary. Top with breadcrumbs and serve immediately.

# LINGUINE CON ALICI FRESCHE, POMODORO E ROSMARINO

## LINGUINE WITH FRESH ANCHOVIES, TOMATOES & ROSEMARY

---

*This is an excellent summer pasta: the combination of fresh fish and ripe tomatoes creates a light and refreshing dish for hot days and nights. This is traditionally considered a Neapolitan dish, but it is also found in the coastal fishing towns of Lazio.*

*Although we often use salt-cured anchovies in other dishes specifically for their robust salty briny taste, this recipe is specifically designed to highlight the delicate flavor of fresh anchovies.*

¼ *cup (60 ml) extra virgin olive oil*

*2 garlic cloves, chopped*

*1 large rosemary sprig, picked and chopped (about 2 teaspoons)*

*2 lbs (907 g) large ripe San Marzano or Roma tomatoes, cored and diced, or cherry tomatoes, cut in half*

*1½ teaspoons hot pepper flakes*

*1 lb (454 g) fresh fileted anchovies*

*1 lb (454 g) linguine*

Bring a large pot of cold water to a boil.

Put the olive oil, garlic, and rosemary in a 14-inch (36-cm) sauté pan over medium-low heat. Cook, stirring occasionally, until the garlic begins to sizzle and is translucent.

Add the diced tomatoes and hot pepper and turn the heat to high. Simmer the tomatoes for 3 minutes until they are soft but still intact.

Carefully layer the fileted anchovies over the tomatoes, season with salt, and turn off the heat. Do not stir, so that the fish cooks whole with the residual heat and breaks into large chunks when you toss it with the pasta (it will break down too quickly if you stir it right away).

Drop the linguine into boiling salted water and cook, stirring frequently, until the pasta is al dente. Drain the linguine, reserving ¼ cup (60 ml) cooking water. Transfer the pasta to the pan, turn the heat to medium-high and toss until well combined, adding cooking water as necessary. Taste and adjust the seasoning and serve immediately.

# BUCATINI CON LE SARDE
## BUCATINI WITH FRESH SARDINES & WILD FENNEL

———

*This is a classic Sicilian dish that I learned from Russell Moore, who was a chef at the Chez Panisse Café for more than 20 years, and is now the chef at Camino in Oakland.*

*We prepare this dish in the spring when one of our farmers, Giovanni Bernabei, forages for wild fennel. Wild fennel is prized for its fronds that resemble dill, but have the pungent aroma and flavor of anise. The unique combination of saffron, wild fennel, and fresh sardines is delicious because these bold flavors manage to stand up to one another and balance each other in perfect harmony.*

¼ cup currants or raisins

¾ cup (177 ml) white wine like a Trebbiano or Grecanico

½ cup (118 ml) extra virgin olive oil

1 medium yellow onion, diced

3 garlic cloves, chopped

1½ teaspoons hot pepper flakes

¼ cup (60 ml) saffron water (see p. 245)

¼ bulb chopped wild fennel

1¾ oz (50 g) pine nuts

3 tablespoons salt-packed capers, rinsed (see p. 244)

30 fresh sardine filets (about 12 oz [340 g])

1 lb (454 g) bucatini or spaghetti

1 cup toasted breadcrumbs (see p. 237)

Plump the currants in ½ cup (118 ml) wine (see p. 244).

Bring a large pot of cold water to a boil.

Put the olive oil and onions in a 14-inch (36-cm) sauté pan over low heat and cook, stirring occasionally, for 10 to 12 minutes, or until the onions are translucent.

Stir in the garlic and hot pepper, and sizzle in the oil for 1 minute. Add ¼ cup (60 ml) white wine and the saffron water and reduce the liquid by three-quarters. Turn off the heat.

When the water comes to a rolling boil, salt it and blanch the wild fennel for about 4 minutes, or until it is tender, then remove it using a slotted spoon.

When the fennel is cool enough to handle, squeeze out any excess water and chop it. Stir in the fennel to the sauté pan along with the currants (reserving the liquid), pine nuts, and capers. Cook for 2 minutes over low heat, then turn off the heat.

Place the sardines in a single layer on top. Do not stir so that the fish cooks whole with the residual heat and breaks into large chunks when you toss it with the pasta (it will break down too quickly if you stir it right away). The sardines should be just barely cooked.

Drop the bucatini into the same boiling salted water and cook, stirring frequently, until the pasta is al dente.

When the pasta is al dente, drain it and transfer the bucatini to the sauté pan. Toss until well combined, adding some currant liquid if the mixture looks dry. Top with breadcrumbs and serve immediately.

# CALAMARATA CON CALAMARI

## CALAMARATA WITH SQUID, RED ONIONS & BREADCRUMBS

———

*There are two slightly different ways to prepare this recipe. One is to sauté the calamari quickly over high heat so that they brown a bit and create a rich fondo, or base, on the bottom of the pan. I prefer this method in winter when it seems more natural to eat richer foods. However, you can also gently sauté the calamari over medium heat for a more delicate flavor, which I prefer in summer.*

*½ cup (118 ml) extra virgin olive oil*

*1 lb (454 g) calamari, cleaned and cut into ¼-inch (.6-cm) rings*

*1 small red onion, diced*

*2 garlic cloves, chopped*

*1½ teaspoons hot pepper flakes*

*3 marjoram sprigs, picked (about 1 teaspoon)*

*15 parsley sprigs, picked and chopped (about 4 tablespoons)*

*1 lb (454 g) calamarata or mezzi rigatoni*

*1 cup toasted breadcrumbs (see p. 237)*

Bring a large pot of cold water to a boil.

Put ¼ cup (60 ml) olive oil in a 14-inch (36-cm) sauté pan over high heat. When hot, add the calamari and sauté for 2 or 3 minutes, until they have wept their juice and cooked down, creating a *fondo*. Remove using a slotted spoon and set them aside.

Add ¼ cup (60 ml) olive oil, red onion, and a pinch of salt to the pan and turn the heat to medium. Cook, stirring frequently, until the onions are translucent. As they sauté, the *fondo* will dissolve and flavor them with the calamari juice, making them look caramelized.

Make a well in the middle of the onions and add the garlic, hot pepper, and herbs. Sizzle in the oil for 1 minute, then turn off the heat and set the pan aside, adding a little cooking water to the pan to halt the frying. Make sure to add the water to the pan away from the heat.

Drop the calamarata into boiling salted water and cook, stirring frequently, until the pasta is al dente. Drain the calamarata and transfer the pasta to the pan right away. Add the calamari and toss until well combined. Top with breadcrumbs and serve immediately.

# GNOCCHETTI SARDI ALLA PALINA

## GNOCCHETTI SARDI WITH CAULIFLOWER, RAISINS, PINE NUTS & SAFFRON ONIONS

*This pasta is Sicilian in origin and is traditionally made with ziti, a long tubular pasta. I prefer to eat this pasta with a* pasta corta, *a short pasta, and I especially like gnocchetti sardi here because of the way they cup the sauce.*

*The sweet mineral taste of the saffron onions is matched against the salty anchovies. This contrast between sweet and savory is very characteristic of Sicilian cuisine. The combination of sour currants plumped in white wine, with the pine nuts and toasted breadcrumbs crumbled over the top, really makes this dish. The key, of course, is a well-made* soffritto *(see p. 35). Make sure you cut the cauliflower florets into very small pieces that match the size of the gnocchetti sardi.*

½ cup currants or raisins

1 cup (237 ml) white wine, like a Trebbiano or Grecanico

¼ cup (60 ml) extra virgin olive oil, plus 2 tablespoons

2 medium yellow onions, cut into ¼-inch (.6-cm) dice

¼ cup (60 ml) saffron water (see p. 245)

1½ lbs (680 g) cauliflower or broccoli romanesco, core removed, cut into ¼-inch (.6-cm) florets

3 garlic cloves, chopped

8 anchovy filets or 4 salt-cured anchovies, cleaned (see p. 244)

1 teaspoon hot pepper flakes

1¾ oz (50 g) pine nuts

Bring a large pot of cold water to a boil.

Plump the currants in the wine (see p. 244).

Put ¼ cup (60 ml) of the olive oil with the onions and a pinch of salt in a 14-inch (36-cm) sauté pan over medium-low heat. After about 8 minutes add the saffron water. Continue cooking, stirring occasionally, until the onions are translucent and turning yellow from the saffron.

Put 2 tablespoons olive oil and ¼ cup (60 ml) water in a separate sauté pan and bring to a boil. Add the cauliflower florets and cover with a lid, stirring frequently and adding cooking water if the pan looks dry. Cook for 15 to 18 minutes, or until the cauliflower florets are very soft.

Make a well in the cauliflower and add the garlic, anchovies, and hot pepper, and sizzle on low heat until the anchovies have broken up and have melted into the oil.

*20 parsley sprigs, picked and chopped (about 6 tablespoons)*

*12 marjoram sprigs, picked and chopped (about 2 teaspoons)*

*1 lb (454 g) gnocchetti sardi*

*1 cup toasted breadcrumbs (see p. 237)*

Stir in the pine nuts, currants (reserving the liquid), saffron onions, parsley, and marjoram, and turn off the heat. Add some currant liquid if the mixture looks dry.

Drop the gnocchetti sardi into boiling salted water and cook, stirring frequently, until the pasta is al dente. Drain the gnocchetti sardi, reserving ¼ cup (60 ml) cooking water. Transfer the pasta to the sauté pan right away and toss until well combined, adding cooking water as necessary. Top with breadcrumbs and serve immediately.

# TROFIE AL PESTO GENOVESE
## TROFIE WITH PESTO, GREEN BEANS & POTATOES

———

*We like to teach our interns "what grows together goes together," which ties in naturally to eating seasonally and sustainably. This philosophy also applies to using specific oils for preparing regional dishes. A classic example of this is pesto Genovese, which should be made with a Ligurian olive oil, praised for its soft, buttery, fruity qualities. If you try to prepare a pesto Genovese with a Tuscan olive oil, it really doesn't work because a Tuscan olive oil, classically grassy and peppery, would overpower the delicate balance of basil, pine nuts, and cheese. The same goes for choosing the cheese: don't use pecorino Romano here, it is far too sharp and salty to lend itself to pesto's subtle combination of flavors. The Genovese prefer to use a more delicate, smooth, and nutty hard grating cheese, like a mild Fiore Sardo or a pecorino Toscano.*

*Traditionally, pasta al pesto was served in Genoa with green beans and potatoes, making it a one-dish meal, but nowadays it is often served without the extra vegetables. We like to make Trofie al Pesto Genovese as a vegetarian main course at dinner in late spring, when basil is just starting to appear in our garden, green garlic has finally reared its head, green beans are at their peak, and new potatoes have arrived with their tender young unformed skins.*

*I always make pesto using a pestle and mortar (see p. 243), but feel free to make the pesto with a hand blender (do not use a food processor because it will not chop the leaves finely enough).*

*1½ oz (43 g) pine nuts*

*½ garlic clove*

*½ cup (118 ml) soft buttery extra virgin olive oil, preferably from Liguria, plus 2 tablespoons*

*80 Italian basil leaves (about 1 large bunch)*

*1 oz (28 g) Fiore Sardo or pecorino Toscano, grated (about ¼ cup)*

Pound the pine nuts in a mortar and pestle, until they have a chunky peanut butter–like consistency, and set them aside.

In the same mortar, pound the garlic with a pinch of salt until you obtain a smooth paste. Set the garlic aside in a small bowl and add 1 or 2 tablespoons of olive oil so that it does not oxidize.

Carefully dice the basil by stacking the leaves one on top of the other and cutting squares with a sharp knife. Work in small batches to avoid discoloring the basil. Pound half of the

2 oz (57 g) Grana Padano, grated
(about ¾ cup),
plus more for serving

1 lb (454 g) trofie

4 oz (113 g) thin green beans,
trimmed and cut in half

1 potato, peeled and cut into
¼-inch (.6-cm) cubes (keep it cut
in cold water until you need it)

basil leaves with a pinch of salt in the mortar. As the basil begins to break down, start using a circular smearing motion to turn the leaves into a paste. Set the basil paste aside and add 1 or 2 tablespoons of olive oil, so that the basil does not turn brown.

Repeat the same process with the rest of the basil.

Combine all of the pounded basil in the mortar and stir in the remaining olive oil and the pine nuts, garlic, pecorino, and Grana and mix until the pesto is smooth. Refrigerate the pesto for 1 hour to allow the flavors to develop. Taste and adjust the seasoning when you're ready to use the pesto.

Bring a large pot of cold water to a boil.

Drop the trofie into boiling salted water. After 6 minutes, drop in the green beans and the potatoes and cook, stirring frequently, until the pasta is al dente. Drain it, reserving ¼ cup (60 ml) cooking water. Transfer the trofie, green beans, potatoes, and pesto to a large bowl and toss until well combined, adding cooking water as necessary. Serve immediately with more freshly grated Grana.

# BAVETTE CON PESCE E PESTO LEGGERO

## BAVETTE WITH WHITE FISH & PESTO

————

*This pasta is an excellent primo for a hot summer day when you want something substantial that is not too heavy. I first tasted this pasta one hot Roman afternoon in July; simple, light, and delicate, this dish was truly a revelation.*

*This recipe is an interesting twist on pesto, or at least on our traditional idea of pesto. It is leggero, or "light," because it doesn't contain any cheese or garlic. This particular combination of fish, herbs, nuts, and olive oil is subtle, clean, and just incredible. And because this pesto has no cheese you may toss it directly in the pan; a pesto that includes cheese should always be tossed in a bowl so that the cheese doesn't coagulate.*

½ cup (118 ml) extra virgin olive oil, plus 2 tablespoons

3½ oz (100 g) pine nuts

1 small bunch parsley, picked and chopped (about ¾ cup)

20 Italian basil leaves

1 lb (454 g) bavette or linguine

½ lb (227 g) sand dabs or other flaky white fish, like haddock, cut into ¼-inch (.6-cm) cubes

Bring a large pot of cold water to a boil.

Put ½ cup olive oil, pine nuts, parsley, basil, and about ½ teaspoon salt in a blender (or use a hand blender) and puree until the mixture is a smooth paste. Taste and adjust the seasoning.

Drop the bavette into boiling salted water and cook, stirring frequently, until the pasta is al dente.

Meanwhile, put 2 tablespoons olive oil and the fish in a 14-inch (36-cm) sauté pan over medium-low heat.

Sauté the fish delicately for 2 to 3 minutes stirring carefully to avoid browning and being careful not to overcook it. Turn off the heat.

When the bavette are al dente, drain the pasta, reserving ¼ cup (60 ml) cooking water. Transfer the bavette right away to the sauté pan with the fish. Add the pesto to the pan and toss until well combined, adding cooking water as necessary. Serve immediately.

# PIZZICHI DI FARINA INTEGRALE CON PESTO DI RUGHETTA

## WHOLE-WHEAT PIZZICHI WITH ARUGULA PESTO

*We like to use farro pasta with arugula pesto, but you can use whole-wheat pasta. The whole-grain flour marries well with the spicy, slightly bitter arugula, the rich toasted walnuts, and the salty pecorino. In the fall, this pasta is delicious with sautéed zucchini and zucchini flowers.*

1½ oz (43 g) walnuts

2 bunches arugula
(about 4 oz [113 g]),
trimmed and chopped

1 oz (28 g) pine nuts

½ garlic clove

¾ cup (177 ml) extra virgin
olive oil,
preferably a soft buttery
olive oil from Liguria

1 oz (28 g) pecorino Romano,
grated (about ¼ cup)

1 oz (28 g) Grana Padano,
grated (about ¼ cup)

1 lb (454 g) pizzichi di farro or
whole-grain penne

Preheat the oven to 300°F (150°C).

Spread the walnuts evenly on a rimmed baking sheet and toast the nuts for 10 minutes, or until the skins begin to split and the nuts are fragrant. While the nuts are still warm, place them inside a clean tea towel. Gather the towel into a secure bundle and roll the nuts in a circular motion to loosen and remove some of the skins, and with them any extra bitterness. Lift the nuts out of the towel, leaving behind the skins.

Put the walnuts, arugula, pine nuts, garlic, and olive oil in a blender and blend until smooth (you may also use a hand blender).

Stir in the pecorino and the Grana. Set the pesto aside for 1 hour to develop its flavors. After 1 hour, taste and adjust the seasoning.

Bring a large pot of cold water to a boil.

Drop the pizzichi into boiling salted water and cook, stirring frequently, until the pasta is al dente. Drain it, reserving ½ cup (118 ml) cooking water. Transfer the pizzichi and pesto to a large mixing bowl and toss well to combine, adding cooking water as necessary. Serve immediately with the remaining Grana.

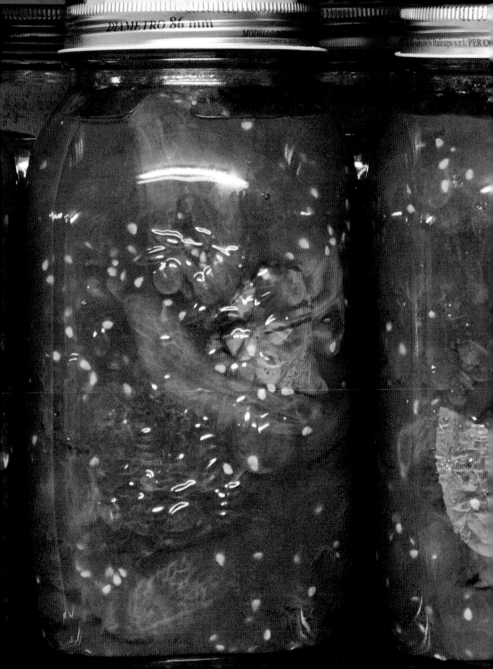

DIAMETRO 86 mm

SUGO

# SUGO

## TOMATO-BASED SAUCES

Learning how to make a *sugo* is the natural next step after *olio* sauces, since tomato sauces directly build off of the *soffritto* technique used for oil-based sauces. Each *sugo* has a *soffritto* at its base, which might even include stewed vegetables or meat.

The recipes in this section are prepared with canned whole San Marzano tomatoes, which get pureed. Do not buy tomatoes that are already pureed; they tend to be watery and have less flavor. Use fresh tomatoes whenever they are in season, but good quality canned San Marzano tomatoes (or San Marzano-style tomatoes) work just as well. Puree them with an immersion blender or in a food processor. The tomato sauces in Sugo made with canned whole San Marzano tomatoes essentially need to simmer for only a short time. This quick simmering time keeps the sauce light, bright, and balanced.

During the summer, however, we like to use fresh tomatoes from the Bass Garden. The sauce needs to cook for a little longer as the fresh tomatoes break down and turn into a sauce (see p. 240 to make sauce from fresh tomatoes). When choosing a fresh tomato for sauce, look for a fleshy, pulpy tomato, such as a San Marzano, Roma, or plum tomato. These varietals make for a full-bodied sauce that coats the pasta generously. Costoluto Genovese or Cuore di Bue tomatoes also make excellent sauces; they are especially delicious in pasta all'Amatriciana, Norma, or Puttanesca, because their slightly higher acidity stands up to the richness of the dish. In late July, when the academic year at the American Academy winds down, we can the San Marzano tomatoes from the Bass Garden to keep for the winter months.

While whole-grain pasta works well with many condiments (specifically with pesto or egg and cheese sauces), it doesn't work with just anything. Whole-grain pasta especially does not pair well with tomato sauces. At the RSFP we believe that the bold flavor of the whole grain interferes with the tomato instead of enhancing the dish.

The secret to a delicious *pasta al sugo* is to drain the pasta a few minutes before it is al dente and to finish cooking it in the sauce over medium-high heat. Instead of absorbing water for the last few minutes of cooking, the pasta absorbs the sauce and imbues the pasta with its flavor.

# PASTA AL POMODORO
## SPAGHETTI WITH TOMATO SAUCE

---

*This is the national dish of Italy. Ironically, despite its supposed simplicity, Pasta al Pomodoro has infinite interpretations; this is how we like to make it. The sauce is technically a* passata—*passed through a sieve—so that it is smooth. We also like to make variations in which we use chopped up canned or fresh tomatoes so the sauce has some texture, or raw pureed tomatoes or stewed cherry tomatoes. Italians like to add half of the basil at the beginning of the cooking process and half at the end so that you taste a broader range of the flavor spectrum.*

¼ cup (60 ml) extra virgin olive oil

3 garlic cloves, smashed

10 Italian basil leaves

1 teaspoon hot pepper flakes

28 oz (794 g) canned whole San Marzano-style tomatoes, pureed with a hand blender or in a food processor

1 lb (454 g) spaghetti

2 oz (57 g) Grana Padano, grated (about ¾ cup)

Bring a large pot of cold water to a boil.

Put the olive oil and garlic in a 14-inch (36-cm) sauté pan over medium-low heat.

When the garlic starts to sizzle, add half of the basil and hot pepper. Cook, stirring occasionally, until the garlic is golden, then remove and discard it.

Add the tomatoes and simmer the sauce until it has reduced by half, and turn off the heat. Add the remaining basil leaves and taste and adjust the seasoning.

Drop the spaghetti into boiling salted water and cook, stirring frequently, until the pasta is almost al dente. Drain the spaghetti 3 minutes before the indicated cooking time, reserving ½ cup (118 ml) cooking water. The pasta will cook for the last few minutes in the sauce and absorb its flavors.

Transfer the spaghetti to the tomato sauce and turn the heat to medium-high. Simmer the pasta in the sauce for about 2 minutes, adding cooking water as necessary and stirring frequently to avoid sticking. Serve immediately with freshly grated Grana.

# PENNE ALL'ARRABBIATA
## PENNE WITH SPICY TOMATO SAUCE

Arrabbiata *in Italian means angry, and this is an "angry" sauce because it is made with Italy's very spicy diavoletti chilies. Alfredo Gianfrocca, the caretaker of Villa Aurelia at the American Academy, used to bring us these chilies from his hometown Frosinone, but we now grow them in the Bass Garden. Fresh or dry chilies may be used in this recipe; we like to use fresh chilies whenever we have them. Just like Pasta al Pomodoro, Penne all'Arrabbiata is an infinitely versatile dish—the important thing is to make it extra spicy.*

*You may also find versions of Penne all'Arrabbiata made with porcini, prosciutto and onions or leeks, or, in Calabria, even with 'nduja, an extremely spicy sausage.*

¼ cup (60 ml) extra virgin olive oil

4 garlic cloves, smashed

1 medium yellow onion, cut into ¼-inch (.6-cm) dice

2 teaspoons hot pepper flakes or 2 fresh red chilies, deseeded and minced

28 oz (794 g) canned whole San Marzano-style tomatoes, pureed with a hand blender or in a food processor

½ teaspoon dried oregano

1 lb (454 g) penne

2 oz (57 g) pecorino Romano, grated (about ½ cup)

Bring a large pot of cold water to a boil.

Put the olive oil, garlic, onion, and a pinch of salt in a 14-inch (36-cm) sauté pan over medium-low heat. Cook, stirring occasionally, until the onions are translucent.

When the garlic is just golden, remove and discard it. Add the hot pepper flakes to the translucent onions and sizzle for 10 to 20 seconds.

Add the tomato puree and simmer the sauce until it has reduced by half. Add the oregano and turn off the heat. Taste and adjust the seasoning.

Drop the penne into boiling salted water and cook, stirring frequently, until the pasta is almost al dente. Drain the penne 3 minutes before the indicated cooking time, reserving ½ cup (118 ml) cooking water. The pasta will cook for the last few minutes in the sauce and absorb its flavors.

Transfer the penne to the tomato sauce and turn the heat to medium-high. Simmer the pasta in the sauce for about 2 minutes, adding cooking water as necessary and stirring frequently to avoid sticking. Serve immediately with freshly grated pecorino.

# PENNE ALLA CHECCA
## PENNE WITH TOMATO SAUCE, FENNEL & PECORINO

*I used to make this tomato-fennel sauce at the Chez Panisse Café when I worked the pizza station. When I came to Italy in 2006, I discovered that there was a similar sauce for pasta called alla checca. At the RSFP we make this version of checca, which is a slight revisiting of the classic dish. We like to use fresh fennel instead of fennel seeds because it imparts a more delicate and subtle anise flavor. The tomato serves as a catalyst to show off the unique combination of fennel, olive, caper, and basil. This pasta is also excellent with sausage added from the start (to make your own see p. 238).*

½ cup (118 ml) extra virgin olive oil

2 small red onions, diced

3 medium fennel bulbs, washed and cut into ½-inch (1.2-cm) dice

25 Italian basil leaves

2 lbs (907 g) fresh San Marzano-style tomatoes, cut in half and pureed

3 garlic cloves, smashed

¼ cup picholine olives or buttery green olives, pitted and chopped

3 tablespoons salt-packed capers, rinsed and chopped (see p. 244)

20 parsley sprigs, picked and chopped (about 6 tablespoons)

1 lb (454 g) penne

2 oz (57 g) pecorino Romano, grated (about ½ cup)

Put ¼ cup of olive oil, red onions, fennel, and a large pinch of salt in a medium pot over medium-high heat. Cook the fennel for about 15 minutes, or until it starts to soften and is slightly translucent. Add the basil and cook for 1 minute more.

Add the tomato puree and simmer the sauce for 40 minutes, or until the fennel is completely tender.

Bring a large pot of cold water to a boil.

When the fennel is completely tender, pass the tomato sauce through a food mill and discard the fibrous leftovers of the fennel and tomato skins, or puree it with a hand blender and pass it through a fine mesh strainer.

Put ¼ cup (60 ml) olive oil, the garlic, olives, and capers in a 14-inch (36-cm) sauté pan over medium heat. Sauté, stirring occasionally, until the garlic is golden and the capers have crisped up a bit. Remove and discard the garlic. Add the parsley, sizzle for 1 minute, and add the tomato sauce. Cook for another minute or two to combine the flavors, and turn off the heat. Taste and adjust seasoning.

Drop the penne into boiling salted water and cook, stirring frequently, until the pasta is almost al dente. Drain the penne 2 minutes before the indicated cooking time, reserving 1 cup (237 ml) cooking water. The pasta will cook for the last few minutes in the sauce and absorb its flavors.

Transfer the penne to the tomato sauce and turn the heat to medium-high. Simmer the pasta in the sauce for 1 to 2 minutes, adding cooking water as necessary and stirring frequently to avoid sticking. Serve immediately with freshly grated pecorino.

# RIGATONI AL SUGO FINTO
## RIGATONI WITH MOCK MEAT SAUCE

---

*A sugo is traditionally a meat-based sauce. Finto in Italian means fake, and in this recipe, the texture and richness of meat is mimicked by the sautéed vegetables and the deep flavor of red wine. We often serve it as a vegetarian alternative for dinner when we make Amatriciana.*

¼ cup (60 ml) extra virgin olive oil

1 celery stalk, cut into ¼-inch (.6-cm) dice

1 medium carrot, cut into ¼-inch (.6-cm) dice

1 medium onion, cut into ¼-inch (.6-cm) dice

6 sage leaves, cut into strips

1 small rosemary sprig, picked and chopped (about 2 teaspoons)

6 marjoram sprigs, picked and chopped (about 2 teaspoons)

20 parsley sprigs, picked and chopped (about 6 tablespoons)

½ cup (118 ml) red wine, like a Cesanese del Piglio

28 oz (794 g) canned whole San Marzano-style tomatoes, pureed with a hand blender or in a food processor

1 lb (454 g) rigatoni

2 oz (57 g) pecorino Romano, grated (about ½ cup)

Bring a large pot of cold water to a boil.

Put the olive oil, celery, carrot, and onion in a 14-inch (36-cm) sauté pan over medium-low heat. Season with salt and cook, stirring occasionally, until the vegetables are translucent and are slightly brown.

Add the herbs and cook for 2 more minutes. Add the red wine and cook until the liquid has reduced by two-thirds.

Add the pureed tomatoes and simmer until the sauce has reduced by half.

Drop the rigatoni into boiling salted water and cook, stirring frequently, until the pasta is almost al dente. Drain the rigatoni 3 minutes before the indicated cooking time, reserving 1 cup (237 ml) cooking water. The pasta will cook for the last few minutes in the sauce and absorb its flavors.

Transfer the rigatoni to the tomato sauce and turn the heat to medium-high. Simmer the pasta in the sauce for about 2 minutes, adding cooking water as necessary and stirring frequently to avoid sticking. Serve immediately with freshly grated pecorino.

# BUCATINI ALL'AMATRICIANA
## BUCATINI WITH TOMATO SAUCE, ONIONS & GUANCIALE

———

*Bucatini all'Amatriciana is a famous Roman pasta, yet it is from Amatrice, near Rieti, on the border of Lazio and Abruzzo.*

*The combination of guanciale and tomato with the addition of pecorino gives this dish its distinctive brick-red color. Amatriciana is traditionally made with bucatini, called as such because the long pasta has a tiny hole in the middle of the noodle that captures sauce and that stands up to the boldness of this rich sauce. Pasta al ceppo is also a delicious substitution for bucatini.*

*One of the various disputes over the many names given to regional dishes is true for Amatriciana as well. While most spell it with the initial A, signaling that it is from Amatrice in Lazio, the dish can also be spelled Matriciana, from Matrice in Molise—it just depends on who you ask!*

*3 tablespoons extra virgin olive oil*

*6 oz (170 g) guanciale, pancetta, or bacon, cut into ½-inch (1.2-cm) dice*

*1 large onion, diced*

*Coarsely ground black pepper, to taste*

*28 oz (794 g) canned whole San Marzano-style tomatoes, pureed with a hand blender or in a food processor*

*1 teaspoon hot pepper flakes*

*1 lb (454 g) bucatini or spaghetti*

*3 oz (85 g) pecorino Romano, grated (about ¾ cup)*

Bring a large pot of cold water to a boil.

Put the olive oil and guanciale in a 14-inch (36-cm) sauté pan over medium-low heat.

After 3 minutes, add the onions. Cook, stirring occasionally, until they are translucent and the guanciale has started to brown. Season with coarsely ground black pepper.

Add the tomatoes and the hot pepper flakes and simmer the sauce until it has reduced by two thirds, then turn off the heat.

Drop the bucatini into boiling salted water and cook, stirring frequently, until the pasta is almost al dente. Drain the bucatini 3 minutes before the indicated cooking time, reserving 1 cup (237 ml) cooking water. The pasta will cook for the last few minutes in the sauce and absorb its flavors.

Transfer the bucatini to the tomato sauce and turn the heat to medium-high. Simmer the bucatini in the sauce for about 2 minutes, adding cooking water as necessary and stirring frequently to avoid sticking.

Transfer the pasta to a large mixing bowl and add half of the pecorino. Toss well until the pasta has turned brick red and serve immediately with the remaining cheese.

# TORTIGLIONI ALLA NORMA

## PASTA WITH TOMATO SAUCE, ROASTED EGGPLANT
## & RICOTTA SALATA

*This is my absolute favorite pasta in the world. In my mind, nothing trumps pasta alla Norma. James Ehrlich was an intern in the summer and fall of 2011. He helped us refine this recipe into what we believe is the ultimate version. Traditionally the eggplant is fried, but at the RSFP we like to roast it, which maintains the integrity of the eggplant flavor while also making the dish much lighter.*

*Sometimes we make a slight variation and add a medley of freshly chopped parsley, basil, and mint at the end.*

1 large Viola or globe eggplant (about 1 to 1-½ lbs [454g to 680 g]), peeled, leaving stripes of skin and cut into ½-inch (1.2-cm) dice

1 cup (237 ml) olive oil

1 medium red onion, thinly sliced

25 Italian basil leaves

1 teaspoon hot pepper flakes

36 oz (1 kg) canned whole San Marzano-style tomatoes, pureed with a hand blender or chopped by hand

1 lb (454 g) tortiglioni or rigatoni

4 oz (113 g) ricotta salata, grated on a box grater using the large holes (about 1½ cups)

In a large mixing bowl, toss the eggplant with ½ cup (118 ml) olive oil and season generously with salt.

Put the eggplant on a baking sheet with parchment paper and roast for 40 to 50 minutes, stirring after 20 minutes, until the eggplant is soft and golden brown.

Meanwhile, put ½ cup olive oil, the onion, and a pinch of salt in a 14-inch (36-cm) sauté pan over medium heat. Cook, stirring occasionally, until the onions are translucent.

Add the basil leaves and the hot pepper to the onions and let sizzle for 30 seconds.

Add the tomato puree and simmer the sauce until it has reduced by half.

When the eggplant is tender and roasted, drop the tortiglioni into boiling salted water and cook, stirring frequently, until the pasta is almost al dente. Drain the tortiglioni 3 minutes before the indicated cooking time, reserving 1 cup (237 ml) cooking water. The pasta will cook for the last few minutes in the sauce and absorb its flavors.

Transfer the pasta and three-quarters of the roasted eggplant to the tomato sauce and turn the heat to medium-high. Simmer the pasta in the sauce for about 2 minutes, adding cooking water as necessary and stirring frequently to avoid sticking. Top with remaining eggplant and freshly grated ricotta salata and serve immediately.

# ORECCHIETTE CON SALSICCIA D'AGNELLO, SALSA DI POMODORO E MENTA

## ORECCHIETTE WITH TOMATO SAUCE, LAMB SAUSAGE & MINT

---

*This is an RSFP invention. We love the combination of tomato sauce and the sausage, especially when we make it ourselves. The beautiful thing about the "little ears," is that they cup the ingredients. Fleck the sausage in the pan to the size of the orecchiette hollows.*

¼ cup (60 ml) extra virgin olive oil

10 oz (283 g) lamb sausage (to make your own see p. 238)

3 garlic cloves, smashed

1 medium red onion, thinly sliced

28 oz (794 g) canned whole San Marzano-style tomatoes, pureed with a hand blender or in a food processor

20 parsley sprigs, picked and chopped (about 6 tablespoons)

12 mint sprigs, picked and chopped (about 4 tablespoons)

1 teaspoon hot pepper flakes

1 lb (454 g) orecchiette

2 oz (57 g) pecorino Romano, grated (about ½ cup)

Bring a large pot of cold water to a boil.

Put the olive oil in a 14-inch (36-cm) sauté pan over medium heat. Add the sausage in small flecks, add the garlic and sauté, stirring frequently, until the sausage starts to brown.

When the garlic is golden, remove and discard it. Add the red onions and a pinch of salt and cook until the onions are translucent.

Add the tomatoes and simmer the sauce until it has reduced by half.

Add the parsley, mint, and hot pepper. Cook for another minute and turn off the heat. Taste and adjust the seasoning.

Drop the orecchiette into boiling salted water and cook, stirring frequently, until the pasta is almost al dente. Drain the orecchiette 3 minutes before the indicated cooking time, reserving 1 cup (237 ml) cooking water. The pasta will cook for the last few minutes in the sauce and absorb its flavors.

Transfer the pasta to the tomato sauce and turn the heat to medium-high. Simmer the pasta in the sauce for about 2 minutes, adding cooking water as necessary and stirring frequently to avoid sticking. Serve immediately with freshly grated pecorino.

# PASTA AL FORNO
## BAKED PASTA WITH TOMATO SAUCE & MOZZARELLA

*At the RSFP we prepare this dish from scratch, often on Friday, which is always family night at the Academy, when many kids come for dinner. However, at home I use this as a way of reinventing leftover pasta. It can be made with virtually any pasta, yet it is best suited for pasta with tomato sauce.*

*If you are preparing this dish from scratch, you don't need to cook the pasta al dente, it can cook a little longer. In fact, this is possibly the only pasta you don't want to cook al dente. Cooking it al dente would dry out the pasta as it bakes in the oven, because the al dente pasta hasn't absorbed all the required moisture.*

*This is an excellent dish to make for dinner parties or large groups of people, because you can prepare it in advance. It's a real crowd pleaser, even for children.*

*I like to add the Grana only when the pasta al forno is fully baked, not before, sprinkling it on at the last minute and leaving the dish in the oven with the door ajar for a few minutes so the Grana can melt.*

1 lb (454 g) rigatoni or any short pasta

1 batch tomato sauce (see p. 69)

1 lb (454 g) mozzarella, cut into ½-inch (1.2-cm) cubes

2 oz (57 g) Grana Padano, grated (about ¾ cup), plus more for serving

Bring a large pot of cold water to a boil.

Drop the pasta into boiling salted water and cook, stirring frequently, until fully cooked (the white line in the middle of the pasta will have disappeared).

Preheat the oven to 400°F (200°C).

Drain the pasta. Transfer it to a large bowl and toss it with the tomato sauce and half of the mozzarella.

Put the pasta in a 9" x 13" (23 cm x 33 cm) ovenproof gratin or baking dish and dot with the rest of the mozzarella.

Bake for 25 minutes, or until the mozzarella has melted and a nice crust has formed.

Remove from the oven and sprinkle with the Grana. Wait 5 minutes for the cheese to melt and serve with more Grana.

# SPAGHETTI ALLA PUTTANESCA
## SPAGHETTI WITH TOMATO SAUCE, ANCHOVIES, CAPERS & OLIVES

———

*Gaeta, on the coast of southern Lazio, is famous for its small round black olives, which, because of their distinct robust flavor and brininess, are essential to making pasta alla puttanesca. There are two schools of thought on how to prepare this dish. Some think the sauce should be stewed and slowly simmered over the course of a few hours, but we believe it is best made as a quick tomato sauce, in which you fry the anchovies and capers in the* soffritto, *quickly stew the tomatoes, and add the olives at the end, which makes for a cleaner and lighter dish. The real trick to a great puttanesca is using the right proportions of ingredients and adding them at specific times, so that each flavor is perfectly distinguishable yet also balanced in the tomato sauce. Don't use any cheese with this pasta; it doesn't go well with anchovies and would ruin the flavor equilibrium.*

*⅓ cup (79 ml) extra virgin olive oil*

*1 medium yellow onion, diced*

*8 to 10 anchovy fillets or 4 to 5 salt-cured anchovies, cleaned (see p. 244)*

*4 tablespoons salt-packed capers, rinsed and chopped (see p. 244)*

*2 teaspoons hot pepper flakes*

*28 oz (794 g) canned whole San Marzano-style tomatoes, pureed with a hand blender or in a food processor*

*½ cup whole Gaeta or oil-cured olives, pitted and chopped*

*½ teaspoon dried oregano*

*1 lb (454 g) spaghetti*

Bring a large pot of cold water to a boil.

Put the olive oil, onion, and a pinch of salt in a 14-inch (36-cm) sauté pan over medium heat. Cook, stirring occasionally, until the onions are translucent.

Make a well in the middle of the onions and add 6 anchovy fillets, the capers, and the hot pepper. Let everything sizzle in the olive oil without stirring. After 2 minutes, stir the anchovies until they have melted and created a nice fishy, salty, spicy oil. Incorporate the anchovies and capers with the onions, stirring well.

Add the tomato puree and simmer the sauce until it has reduced by half.

Add the other 2 anchovy fillets, the olives, and the dried oregano and simmer for 2 more minutes, then turn off the heat.

Drop the spaghetti into boiling salted water and cook, stirring frequently, until the pasta is almost al dente. Drain the spaghetti 3 minutes before the indicated cooking time, reserving ½ cup (118 ml) cooking water. The pasta will cook for the last few minutes in the sauce and absorb its flavors.

Transfer the spaghetti to the tomato sauce and turn the heat to medium-high. Simmer the pasta in the sauce for about 2 minutes, adding cooking water as necessary and stirring frequently to avoid sticking. Serve immediately.

# RIGATONI CON LA PAIATA

## RIGATONI WITH MILK-FED LAMB INTESTINES, TOMATO SAUCE, MARJORAM & SWEET SPICES

———

*Rigatoni con la paiata originated in the Testaccio neighborhood, where the slaughter-houses of Rome once existed. An animal is broken down into quarters, and the remaining "undesirable" parts of the animal make up the fifth quarter. Testaccio cuisine is famous for using this fifth quarter—all the innards, heart, liver, lung, intestine, and brain.*

*Paiata is the intestine of a milk-fed spring lamb or calf. It is important that the animal has not started eating anything other than its mother's milk. During the cooking process this milk naturally curdles and turns into ricotta. The intestines are tied into sausage-type links to hold in the milk. Once the links are cooked and untied, the ricotta mixes in with the tomato sauce and you are left with a creamy and uniquely spiced sauce.*

*1 lb (454 g) milk-fed veal or lamb intestines*

*1 tablespoon extra virgin olive oil*

*4 oz (113 g) lardo or prosciutto fat, cut into ¼-inch (.6-cm) dice*

*2 garlic cloves, smashed*

*10 marjoram sprigs, picked and chopped (about 2 teaspoons)*

*1 large rosemary sprig, picked and chopped (about 2 tablespoons)*

*2 whole cloves*

*Pinch cinnamon*

*1½ teaspoons hot pepper flakes*

*½ cup (118 ml) dry white wine, preferably from the Castelli Romani*

Carefully cut the intestines into small 3- or 4-inch (8- or 10-cm) links, bring the ends together, and tie them to form a ring.

Put the olive oil and prosciutto fat in a 14-inch (36-cm) sauté pan over low heat and cook until the fat is translucent.

Add the garlic, marjoram, rosemary, cloves, cinnamon, and hot pepper and sizzle in the oil for 2 minutes.

Add the *paiata*, and slowly allow the links to brown with the *soffritto*, stirring occasionally and turning the links over gently once they are browned on one side.

Add the white wine and let the liquid reduce by two-thirds.

Add the tomato puree and cover the pan with a lid. Simmer the sauce for about 1 hour and 45 minutes, or until the *paiata* is tender, then turn off the heat. You should meet very little resistance when you poke the links with a fork.

*28 oz (794 g) canned whole San Marzano-style tomatoes, pureed with a hand blender or in a food processor*

*1 lb (454 g) rigatoni*

*2 oz (57 g) pecorino Romano, grated (about ½ cup)*

Bring a large pot of cold water to a boil.

When the *paiata* is tender, carefully cut and remove the strings tying the intestines and cut each link in half with scissors. Stir well so that the *paiata* "ricotta" mixes with the sauce.

Drop the rigatoni into boiling salted water and cook, stirring frequently, until the pasta is almost al dente. Drain the rigatoni 3 minutes before the indicated cooking time, reserving 1 cup (237 ml) cooking water. The pasta will cook for the last few minutes in the sauce and absorb its flavors.

Transfer the pasta to the tomato sauce and turn the heat to medium-high. Simmer the pasta in the sauce for about 2 minutes, adding cooking water as necessary and stirring frequently to avoid sticking. Serve immediately with freshly grated pecorino.

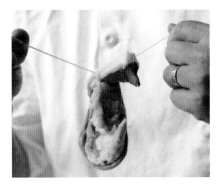

# SPAGHETTI CON SUGO DI POLPETTE
## SPAGHETTI & MEATBALLS

*Spaghetti and meatballs is a fantastic family night dish at the Academy. It's easy to make ahead and perfect for a Sunday lunch or for dinner parties. Meatballs can be made in several different ways, with or without tomato sauce. They can be browned in a pan, deep-fried, or cooked directly in tomato sauce. If they are made in the sauce, the tomato sauce is used to coat the pasta as the* primo, *and the meatballs themselves are served as the* secondo. *We like to serve the meatballs this way at the RSFP.*

½ cup (118 ml) extra virgin olive oil

1 batch meatballs (see p. 90)

3 garlic cloves, smashed

44 oz (1.25 kg) canned whole San Marzano-style tomatoes, pureed with a hand blender or in a food processor

20 Italian basil leaves

1 teaspoon hot pepper flakes

1 lb (454 g) spaghetti

2 oz (57 g) Grana Padano, grated (about ¾ cup)

Prepare the meatballs (see the next page).

Put the olive oil in a 14-inch (36-cm) high-sided sauté pan over medium heat.

When the oil is hot, gently fry the meatballs for 3 or 4 minutes on one side, or until they are golden brown. Carefully turn the meatballs over using a small spatula or spoon and add the garlic. Cook until the garlic is golden, then remove and discard it.

When the meatballs are golden brown, add the tomato puree, basil, and hot pepper flakes, and cook, covered with a lid, for 50 minutes (add some water if the meatballs aren't submerged in tomato sauce) or until the meatballs are very tender.

Bring a large pot of cold water to a boil.

Drop the spaghetti into boiling salted water and cook, stirring frequently, until the pasta is almost al dente.

Meanwhile, remove almost all the meatballs from the sauce and set them aside on a plate. Leave 2 or 3 meatballs in the sauce so they break up when you toss the pasta.

Drain the spaghetti 3 minutes before the indicated cooking time, reserving ½ cup (118 ml) cooking water. The pasta will cook for the last few minutes in the sauce and absorb its flavors.

Transfer the spaghetti to the tomato sauce and turn the heat to medium-high. Simmer the pasta in the sauce for about 2 minutes, adding cooking water as necessary and stirring frequently to avoid sticking. Top with the meatballs if you like and serve immediately with freshly grated Grana.

# POLPETTE

## MEATBALLS

---

*Meatballs are originally a food of the poor because they were made with mostly stale bread soaked in milk with the addition of any meat scraps on hand. Today, meatballs in Italy still contain lots of bread—and are thus quite light. In fact, our meatballs are made with equal parts bread and meat.*

*This recipe works best with bread that is at least 2 to 3 days old—but day-old bread will work. Using stale bread that has been rehydrated allows it to crumble nicely and become flaky.*

*10 oz (283 g) day-old rustic country bread, crust removed and cut into 1-inch (2.5-cm) cubes*

*2 cups (473 ml) whole milk*

*½ lb (227 g) ground beef*

*½ lb (227 g) ground pork*

*Freshly ground black pepper, to taste*

*1 teaspoon hot pepper flakes*

*½ teaspoon dried oregano*

*20 parsley sprigs, picked and chopped (about 6 tablespoons)*

*½ garlic clove, pounded (see p. 244)*

*2 oz (57 g) Grana Padano, grated (about ¾ cup)*

*1 egg*

Put the bread and the milk in a large bowl so that the bread is fully submerged in milk and soak it for 45 minutes.

Season the ground meat with salt and pepper. Add the hot pepper, oregano, parsley, garlic, Grana, and egg to the meat and mix thoroughly using your hands, and set it aside until the soaked bread is ready to use.

Squeeze the milk out of the bread and discard the liquid. Crumble the soaked bread using your thumb and forefingers into the ground meat mixture. Knead the bread and meat mixture. Once this *impasto* comes together, knead it a few more times as if you were kneading fresh pasta (see p. 154).

Form the mix into small balls, about the size of a golf ball, and proceed with the Spaghetti and Meatballs recipe.

VERDURE

# VERDURE

## VEGETABLE-BASED SAUCES

This section is truly ingredient-driven. It is perhaps the most varied section in the book, in terms of both how to prepare the sauces and how to cook the pasta with them. The diversity of this section stems from the range of the vegetables themselves. The *soffritto* plays an important underlying role here, too—it allows the vegetables to take center stage.

It is crucial to understand how to exalt the flavor of each vegetable, and how the right preparation and proper cooking technique will allow you to obtain the texture that highlights the natural qualities of each vegetable.

A few dishes are delicious made with raw vegetables, some need the vegetables blanched, while others use vegetables that are cooked a bit longer. Most Italian pasta recipes with vegetables require that the vegetables first be blanched and then sautéed in the *soffritto*, thereby combining various cooking techniques and uniting the flavors of the *soffritto* with those of the vegetables. Some pasta dishes are cooked for the last few minutes in the sauce (same technique as with tomato sauces) while others are simply tossed with the vegetables (just like with the oil recipes). Making pasta with vegetables is about being familiar with these different preparations and cooking techniques, while also being able to be flexible and constantly respond to the vegetable at hand.

The rhythm of each season directly affects the quality and character of the vegetable. It will largely dictate how the dish will need to be constructed as the season evolves. I explain these seasonal changes in the recipes so you can adapt them accordingly, but use your judgment to understand whether something needs to be cooked more or less in order to extract its delicious flavor. Let your ingredients determine how you will prepare them and respect the seasonality and the individuality of your *materia prima*.

# PENNE ALLA NONNA DI CHIARA
## PENNE WITH BROCCOLI ROMANESCO & PECORINO

———

*Broccoli Romanesco is to my mind one of the most beautiful and mathematically perfect vegetables. Its light-green points are arranged in a pattern known as Fibonacci's sequence.*

*Chiara Bencivenga was one of our Roman interns in the fall of 2010. This is a recipe from her Neapolitan grandmother. This simple dish of boiled broccoli Romanesco, combined with the right green grassy resinous olive oil and sharp pecorino Romano, is just fantastic. Despite its name, broccoli Romanesco is much more like cauliflower than regular broccoli. If you can't find Romanesco, use cauliflower.*

*1 head broccoli Romanesco or cauliflower (about 2 lbs [907 g]), cut into ½-inch (1.2-cm) florets*

*1 lb (454 g) penne*

*½ cup (118 ml) extra virgin olive oil*

*½ teaspoon hot pepper flakes*

*2 oz (57 g) pecorino Romano, grated (about ½ cup)*

Bring a large pot of cold water to a boil.

When the water comes to a rolling boil, salt it, and drop the broccoli Romanesco. After 8 minutes, add the penne and cook, stirring frequently, until the pasta is al dente.

Put the olive oil and hot pepper flakes in a large mixing bowl.

When the pasta is al dente, drain it and transfer the penne and Romanesco to the bowl. Toss until the pasta is coated with the olive oil, top with lots of pecorino and serve immediately.

# CONCHIGLIE AL POMODORO CRUDO
## CONCHIGLIE WITH RAW TOMATO SAUCE

*This pasta is sublime on hot days because the raw tomato is so refreshing. This dish also makes for a great pasta salad, enjoyed at room temperature or even cold.*

*The tomatoes should be a little acidic, so choosing the right tomato varietal is key: use an Early Girl tomato or a nice ripe cherry tomato. Add a splash of red wine vinegar to the tomatoes if they seem too sweet or taste flat. If you puree the tomatoes with the olive oil, the sauce will turn orange. To keep the raw tomato a vibrant red, make sure you puree the tomatoes first and only then add the olive oil.*

*2 lbs (907 g) ripe red Early Girl tomatoes, cored and cut in quarters, or ripe cherry tomatoes, cut in half*

*15 Italian basil leaves*

*⅓ cup (79 ml) extra virgin olive oil*

*1 tablespoon red wine vinegar, optional*

*½ teaspoon hot pepper flakes*

*1 lb (454 g) conchiglie or shell-shaped pasta*

*4 oz (113 g) ricotta salata, grated on a box grater using the large holes (about 1½ cups)*

Bring a large pot of cold water to a boil.

Puree the tomatoes with the basil in a blender or in a bowl using a hand blender, then add the olive oil and the hot pepper (see headnote). Taste and adjust the seasoning with salt and red wine vinegar if the sauce is too sweet or tastes flat.

Drop the conchiglie into boiling salted water and cook, stirring frequently, until the pasta is al dente. Drain it, transfer the conchiglie to a large bowl, and toss with the raw tomato sauce. Serve with freshly grated ricotta salata.

# FUSILLI CON PESTO DI CAVOLO NERO

## FUSILLI WITH KALE PESTO

*Domenico Cortese, a cook at the RSFP for more than three years, introduced me to this very special dish. I consider it a pesto because of the way in which it is made, but the combination of flavors is entirely unique. Here, the herbs used in a classic pesto are replaced with cavolo nero (Tuscan kale) and potatoes replace most of the nuts traditionally used to help bind the pesto. The lemon juice and zest are surprising additions that really brighten the dish. To top it all off, cavolo nero is incredibly nutritious and rich in vitamins A and C. Make sure you use Tuscan or Lacinato kale with their large sturdy rippled dark green leaves.*

*1 oz (28 g) walnuts*

*1 lb (454 g) Tuscan or Lacinato kale, leaves stripped from the stems*

*2 oz (57 g) potatoes (about ½ potato), peeled and diced*

*⅔ cup (158 ml) extra virgin olive oil*

*2½ garlic cloves*

*10 parsley sprigs, picked and chopped (about 3 tablespoons)*

*1 or two strips lemon peel*

*1 lb (454 g) fusilli*

*1½ teaspoons freshly squeezed lemon juice*

*3 oz (85 g) ricotta salata, grated on a box grater using the large holes (about 1 cup)*

Preheat the oven to 400°F (200°C).

Bring a medium pot of cold water to a boil.

Spread the walnuts evenly on a rimmed baking sheet and toast them for 10 minutes, or until the skins begin to split and the nuts are fragrant. While the nuts are still warm, place them inside a clean tea towel. Gather the towel into a secure bundle and roll the nuts in a circular motion to loosen and remove some of the skins, and with them any extra bitterness. Lift the nuts out of the towel, leaving behind the skins.

When the water comes to a rolling boil, salt it, and blanch the kale until it is tender. Remove it using a slotted spoon and spread it out on a baking sheet. Blanch the potatoes until they are tender and the edges are fuzzy, and spread them out on a baking sheet.

When the kale is cool enough to handle, squeeze it to remove excess water and chop it.

Put 2 tablespoons olive oil and 2 garlic cloves in a 14-inch (36-cm) sauté pan over medium heat. When the garlic is golden, remove and discard it. Add the kale and the potatoes. Sauté for 3 or 4 minutes and turn off the heat.

When the kale and potatoes have cooled, put them in a blender (or in a bowl using a hand blender), add the parsley, olive oil, ½ garlic clove, walnuts, lemon peel. Taste and adjust the seasoning, then add the Grana.

Drop the fusilli into boiling salted water and cook, stirring frequently, until the pasta is al dente. Drain it, reserving ¼ cup (60 ml) cooking water. Transfer the fusilli and pesto to a large bowl and add the lemon juice. Toss until well combined, adding cooking water as necessary. Serve immediately with ricotta salata.

# PASTA E LENTICCHIE
## DITALINI WITH LENTILS, ROSEMARY & RICOTTA SALATA

*I absolutely love Pasta e Lenticchie. Mona Talbott, the former executive chef of the RSFP, makes the best pasta e lenticchie I've ever had. We both go crazy for the combination of earthy lentils with rosemary and ricotta salata. There are two ways to cook this pasta, as a dense soup or sautéed. Mona and I both prefer to make this dish with a little less liquid, so sautéed. There are many different varieties of lentils. The lentils we use at the RSFP for this pasta are the lenticchie di Castelluccio, a small brown lentil that has an earthy, slightly cinnamon-like quality.*

½ cup (118 ml) extra virgin olive oil

1 celery stick, cut into ¼-inch (.6-cm) dice

1 small yellow onion, cut into ¼-inch (.6-cm) dice

2 oz (57 g) prosciutto di parma, cut into ¼-inch (.6-cm) dice

1½ cups Castelluccio lentils, or other brown lentils

2 garlic cloves, chopped

1 large rosemary sprig, picked and chopped (about 2 tablespoons)

20 parsley sprigs, picked and chopped (about 6 tablespoons)

1 teaspoon hot pepper flakes

1 lb (454 g) ditalini

4 oz (113 g) ricotta salata, grated on a box grater using the large holes (about 1½ cups)

Put ¼ cup (60 ml) olive oil, celery, onion, and prosciutto in a medium-size pot over medium heat. Sauté until the onion is translucent and the mix is just starting to color.

Add the lentils and cover with 5 cups water. Slowly simmer over low heat until the lentils are tender, about 35 to 45 minutes. Do not boil the lentils, or they will split. Once the lentils have cooled completely, drain them, reserving all of the lentil water.

Bring a large pot of cold water to a boil.

In a separate pan, make the soffritto: put ¼ cup (60 ml) olive oil, garlic, and rosemary in a 14-inch (36-cm) high sided sauté pan over low heat. When the garlic is just golden, add the parsley and hot pepper; sizzle for 30 seconds and add the lentils along with 1½ cups lentil water to the soffritto (continue to reserve the remaining lentil liquid for later). Taste and adjust seasoning.

Drop the ditalini into boiling salted water and cook, stirring frequently, until the pasta is almost al dente.

Drain the ditalini 3 minutes before the indicated cooking time. The pasta will cook for the last few minutes in the sauce and absorb its flavors. Transfer the ditalini to the lentils and cook for 3 more minutes, stirring occasionally, until the mixture thickens. Add more of the lentil cooking liquid if the mixture looks too thick. Serve immediately with freshly grated ricotta salata.

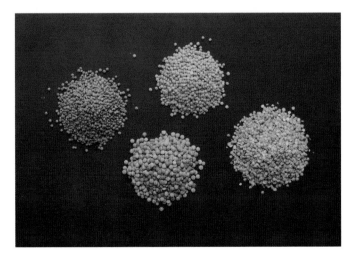

# ORECCHIETTE CON CAVOLFIORE, ACCIUGHE E ROSMARINO

## ORECCHIETTE WITH CAULIFLOWER, ANCHOVIES, GARLIC & ROSEMARY

*This dish was eye opening for me. I never loved cauliflower until I tasted it prepared in this way. I was blown away by the competing flavors that bring out the best in the cauliflower. This dish is basically cauliflower alla Romana, which is slow-cooked cauliflower paired with the bold flavors of anchovies, rosemary, and hot pepper, and served with orecchiette.*

*1 whole cauliflower (about 2 lbs [907 g]), cut into ½-inch (1.2-cm) florets*

*½ cup (118 ml) extra virgin olive oil*

*3 garlic cloves, chopped*

*8 anchovy filets or 4 salt-cured anchovies, cleaned (see p. 244)*

*1 large rosemary sprig, picked and chopped (about 2 tablespoons)*

*1½ teaspoons hot pepper flakes*

*1 lb (454 g) orecchiette*

*1 cup toasted breadcrumbs (see p. 237)*

*2 oz (57 g) Grana Padano, grated (about ¾ cup)*

Bring a large pot of cold water to a boil.

When the water comes to a rolling boil, salt it and drop the cauliflower. Blanch for 5 minutes and remove it using a slotted spoon, reserving water. Spread it out on a baking sheet to cool.

Put the olive oil and cauliflower in a 14-inch (36-cm) sauté pan over medium-high heat. Cook, stirring occasionally, until the cauliflower is soft and falling apart.

Make a well in the cauliflower and add the garlic, anchovies, rosemary, and hot pepper to the pan. Cook, stirring occasionally, until the garlic is golden, then turn off the heat. Taste and adjust the seasoning.

Drop the orecchiette into boiling salted cauliflower water and cook, stirring frequently, until the pasta is al dente. Drain the orecchiette, reserving ¼ cup (60 ml) cooking water. Transfer the pasta to the pan and toss well until the cauliflower sauce has thoroughly coated the pasta, adding cooking water if necessary. Top with breadcrumbs and serve immediately with freshly grated Grana.

# ORECCHIETTE CON PATATE E RUGHETTA
## ORECCHIETTE WITH FRIED POTATOES & ARUGULA

—

*Giovanni Bernabei is an organic farmer from near Frosinone who supplies us with the fantastic potatoes that absolutely make this dish. His potatoes have a dense flesh, deep yellow color, and excellent starch content that is ideal for making gnocchi, gratins, or this pasta. Yukon gold potatoes most closely resemble Giovanni's potatoes.*

*This dish is of Puglian origin, where it is often served as a one-dish meal. The potatoes are traditionally boiled, but I like frying them so they get a little crispy.*

2 medium Yukon gold potatoes, cut into ½-inch (1.2-cm) cubes

⅓ cup (79 ml) extra virgin olive oil

1 medium red onion, cut into ¼-inch (.6-cm) dice

3 garlic cloves, chopped

1 large rosemary sprig, picked and chopped (about 2 tablespoons)

2 teaspoons hot pepper flakes or 1 teaspoon fresh hot red pepper, deseeded and chopped

4 oz (113 g) arugula (about 2 bunches), trimmed and cut in half lengthwise if the leaves are long

1 lb (454 g) orecchiette

2 oz (57 g) pecorino Romano, grated (about ½ cup)

Bring a large pot of cold water to a boil.

When the water comes to a rolling boil, salt it and cook the potatoes for 6 minutes, or until the edges are fuzzy. Remove them using a slotted spoon and spread the potatoes out on a baking sheet, reserving water.

When the potatoes are cool, put the olive oil in a 14-inch (36-cm) sauté pan over medium heat. Once the oil is hot, add the potatoes and cook, stirring occasionally, until they start to crisp up.

Add the red onions and cook until they are translucent.

Make a well in the onions and add the garlic, rosemary, hot pepper, and half of the arugula. Sizzle for 1 minute, then turn off the heat and set the pan aside. Taste and adjust the seasoning.

Drop the orecchiette into the boiling salted potato water and cook, stirring frequently, until the pasta is al dente. Drain it, transfer the orecchiette to the sauté pan, and toss until well combined. Top with the remaining arugula and serve immediately with freshly grated pecorino.

# GARGANELLI CON FAVE FRESCHE, CICORIA E RICOTTA SALATA

## GARGANELLI WITH FRESH FAVA BEANS, DANDELION GREENS & RICOTTA SALATA

---

*Fava beans and dandelion greens is a classic Puglian combination. Legend has it that Hercules was from Puglia, and that these foods helped him become strong in his youth.*

*If you are preparing this dish in early spring, when fava beans are young and tender, omit the dandelion greens—they overpower the fava's delicate flavor. As the season progresses and the weather gets warmer, the fava beans get bigger and starchier. These starchier fava beans start to fall apart when cooked and form a puree. Garganelli is a very unique quill-shaped pasta similar to penne rigate, but handmade with egg and flour.*

½ cup (118 ml) extra virgin olive oil

½ bunch green garlic, green part removed and white part cut into ¼-inch (.6-cm) dice (about 1 cup)

2 cups shelled fava beans (about 3 to 4 lbs [1.4 to 1.8 kg] unshelled)

1 teaspoon hot pepper flakes

1 large rosemary sprig, picked and chopped (about 2 tablespoons)

½ lb (227 g) dandelion greens

1 lb (454 g) garganelli

4 oz (113 g) ricotta salata, grated (about 1½ cups)

Bring a large pot of cold water to a boil.

Bring a medium pot of water to a boil.

When the water in the medium pot comes to a rolling boil, salt it and blanch the dandelion greens until they are very tender. Remove them using a slotted spoon and spread them out on a baking sheet.

Add the fava beans to the same water and cook for 45 seconds. Remove the fava beans using a slotted spoon and transfer them to a bowl of ice water. Peel the fava beans by removing and discarding the tough and slightly bitter outer layer and gently squeezing out the two lobed bright green beans inside. If the fava beans are very small, you don't have to peel them.

Put the olive oil and green garlic in a 14-inch (36-cm) high-sided sauté pan over medium-low heat. Cook, stirring occasionally, until the garlic is golden brown.

Add the fava beans, a pinch of salt, hot pepper, and rosemary and continue cooking over medium heat until the fava beans are soft, tender, and breaking down. If you are using late season fava beans that are slightly starchy, add 1 cup (237 ml) water to help them break down, adding more water if necessary, until they form a puree, with some fava pieces remaining, and turn off the heat. (If the fava beans aren't breaking down, use a hand blender to puree them a bit.)

When the dandelion greens are cool enough to handle, squeeze out any excess water and roughly chop them.

Drop the garganelli into the large pot of boiling salted water and cook, stirring frequently, until the pasta is almost al dente.

Meanwhile, add the dandelion greens to the sauté pan (if you're using them) and turn the heat to medium. Cook for 1 minute and turn off the heat. Taste and adjust the seasoning.

Drain the garganelli 1 minute before the indicated cooking time, reserving ¼ cup (60 ml) cooking water. The pasta will cook for the last minute in the sauce and absorb its flavors.

Transfer the pasta to the sauté pan and turn the heat to medium. Simmer the pasta in the sauce for 1 minute, adding cooking water as necessary and stirring frequently to avoid sticking. Serve immediately with freshly grated ricotta salata.

# MAIALE

## PORK

We often joke in the RSFP kitchen that in Italy, pork is considered a vegetable. As ironic as this may seem, you'll find pork bits in many a vegetable dish. Most will agree: pork just makes everything taste better. So talking about pork amidst vegetable recipes is strangely appropriate.

At the RSFP we believe that the best pork in Italy comes from Cinta Senese pigs. Throughout history the Cinta Senese has been praised for its perfectly marbled meat and succulent flavor. This uniquely marbled meat is also topped with a delicious thick fat cap. Cinta is ideal for making cured meats like guanciale, lardo, and pancetta. It is also excellent for making sausages or braising and roasting, since the marbled meat bastes itself from within as it slowly cooks.

Cinta Senese pigs have existed in Tuscany since the fourteenth century, but the breed can be traced back to Ancient Roman or even Etruscan times. These pigs owe their name to the white belt (*cinta*) that runs across their shoulders and front legs, and to the hills of Siena in Tuscany in which they are raised. Cinta pigs are very active, requiring lots of land to roam free. They also need at least 18 months to reach full size (310 lbs [140 kg]), which is a long time for such a small pig.

Until the middle of the twentieth century, Cinta Senese pigs were very popular in the Tuscan hills. Yet by the late 1950s not only had the overall demand for meat increased as Italy became wealthier, but Italians also suddenly wanted leaner cuts. In response to these demands, new and different breeds of pigs were selected (such as the Large White pig) because they grew larger, more rapidly, bred more and did so faster, stayed leaner, and needed less space to roam. The Cinta breed quickly fell out of favor and was in danger of extinction. Some estimated that by 1986, fewer than 100 Cinta pigs were left. In the last 25 years, dedicated breeders have learned to appreciate and value the unique qualities of this special breed. The revival of the Cinta Senese has played an important role in reestablishing heritage pork breeding in Italy and around the globe. Cinta Senese meat has slowly but surely regained popularity and was awarded a D.O.P. classification in 2012.

Whenever possible, seek out local heritage pork breeds from small farms for the most flavorful, equitable, and highest-quality meat.

# ORECCHIETTE CON BROCCOLETTI E SALSICCIA

## ORECCHIETTE WITH BROCCOLI RAAB & SAUSAGE

*Ask anyone who's tasted it: this is an amazing pasta. It really is in everyone's top five favorites. Just try it.*

¼ cup (60 ml) extra virgin olive oil

10 oz (283 g) pork sausage (to make your own see p. 238)

1 medium red onion, thinly sliced

3 garlic cloves, smashed

1½ teaspoons hot pepper flakes

1 to 1½ lbs (454 to 680 g) broccoli raab, stems trimmed

1 lb (454 g) orecchiette

2 oz (57 g) pecorino Romano, grated (about ½ cup)

Bring a large pot of cold water to a boil.

Put the olive oil in a 14-inch (36-cm) sauté pan over medium-low heat. Add the sausage to the pan in small flecks the size of the orecchiette hollows and cook, stirring occasionally, until the sausage is browned and slightly crispy.

Add the onions, garlic, and hot pepper and cook until the onions are translucent. Turn off the heat and set the pan aside.

When the water comes to a rolling boil, salt it, and blanch the broccoli raab until it is tender. Remove it using a slotted spoon (reserving the broccoli raab water) and spread it out on a baking sheet to cool. When cool enough to handle, squeeze out any excess water and roughly chop the broccoli raab. Add it to the sauté pan and turn the heat to medium. Stir well to combine the ingredients and cook for 3 more minutes, then turn off the heat.

Adjust the salt of the broccoli raab water and drop the orecchiette into the boiling water. Cook, stirring frequently, until the pasta is almost al dente. The pasta will cook for the last few minutes in the sauce and absorb its flavors.

Drain the orecchiette 2 minutes before the indicated cooking time, reserving ½ cup

(118 ml) cooking water. Transfer the pasta to the sauté pan, and turn the heat to high. Cook for 2 more minutes, adding cooking water as necessary and stirring frequently to avoid sticking. Serve immediately with freshly grated pecorino.

# STROZZAPRETI CON CAROTE E SALSICCIA
## STROZZAPRETI WITH CARROTS, SAUSAGE & ROSEMARY

———

*The idea for this recipe came from Cristina Puglisi, deputy director of the American Academy. It has been in her family for years. I was skeptical at first: while the flavors of carrots, bay leaves, and sausage go well together, adding these ingredients to pasta sounded strange, even to an American. Cristina and I made it together a few years ago, and I was so impressed. I really like it with a little rosemary and yellow onions as well. It works, and to top it off the carrots imbue the oil with a beautiful orange hue.*

*2 tablespoons extra virgin olive oil*

*10 oz (283 g) pork sausage (to make your own see p. 238)*

*1 small yellow onion, diced*

*¼ cup (60 ml) white wine, preferably a Soave*

*2 bay leaves*

*1 rosemary sprig, picked and chopped (about 1 tablespoon)*

*5 fresh carrots with tops on, peeled and grated on a box grater using the large holes*

*Freshly ground black pepper, to taste*

*1 lb (454 g) penne*

*2 oz Grana Padano, grated (about ¾ cup), optional*

Bring a large pot of cold water to a boil.

Put the olive oil in a 14-inch (36-cm) sauté pan over medium-low heat.

Crumble the sausage directly into the sauté pan and cook until the sausage has started to brown and is slightly crisp all over. Add the bay and rosemary, let sizzle for 30 seconds, add the onion and cook, stirring occasionally, until it is translucent. Add the white wine and cook until the liquid has evaporated. Add the grated carrots along with lots of black pepper. Sauté for 2 to 3 minutes, mixing well. Add a cup of almost boiling cooking water. Cover the sauté pan and cook for 20 minutes, or until the carrots are very tender. If the pan looks dry, add more water. Taste and adjust the seasoning.

Drop the penne into boiling salted water and cook, stirring frequently, until the pasta is almost al dente.

Drain it 2 minutes before the indicated cooking time, reserving ¼ cup (60 ml) cooking water. The pasta will cook for the last few minutes in the sauce and absorb its flavors.

Transfer the penne to the sauté pan and turn the heat to medium-high. Simmer the pasta in the sauce for about 2 minutes, adding cooking water as necessary and stirring frequently to avoid sticking. Serve immediately with freshly grated Grana, if you like.

# RUOTE CON PEPERONI E SALSICCIA
## RUOTE WITH RED PEPPERS & SAUSAGE

*Peppers thrive in Italy's volcanic soil. Peppers and basil is a classic combination, which provides sweetness that contrasts well with the salty sausage. This pasta works best with a thick-fleshed pepper that stands up to the texture of the pasta. Each different pepper has a specific flavor profile ranging from very sweet to extremely spicy—feel free to mix different types of peppers to taste this range of flavors. At the American Academy, we like to mix in fresh hot peppers from the Bass Garden.*

¼ cup (60 ml) extra virgin olive oil

10 oz (283 g) pork sausage (to make your own see p. 238)

3 garlic cloves, smashed

2 large thick-flesh heirloom red peppers (about 1 lb [454 g]), seeded and small-diced

1 fresh red hot pepper, deseeded and minced, or 1 teaspoon hot pepper flakes

25 Italian basil leaves, torn

1 tablespoon red wine vinegar, optional

1 lb (454 g) ruote or rotelle

2 oz (57 g) pecorino Romano, grated (about ½ cup)

Bring a large pot of cold water to a boil.

Put the olive oil in a 14-inch (36-cm) sauté pan over medium-low heat. Crumble the sausage directly into the pan and cook, stirring occasionally, until the sausage is browned and slightly crispy.

Add the garlic and red peppers and begin to stew them for at least 20 minutes, stirring frequently, until the peppers are very tender.

Add the hot pepper and the torn basil and sizzle for 1 minute, then turn off the heat and set the pan aside. Taste and adjust the seasoning with red wine vinegar if the peppers taste too sweet.

Drop the ruote into boiling salted water and cook, stirring frequently, until the pasta is al dente. Drain it and transfer the ruote to the pan. Toss until well combined and serve immediately with freshly grated pecorino.

# FARFALLE CON ZUCCHINE E 'NDUJA

## FARFALLE WITH ZUCCHINI & SPICY PORK SAUSAGE

*Domenico Cortese, a cook at the RSFP from Tropea, introduced us to this spicy Calabrian sausage called 'nduja, a soft spreadable sausage cured with lots of fresh hot chilies. Because they are high in ascorbic acid, the chilies serve as natural preservatives. The diavoletti chilies used for 'nduja have an intense pepper flavor, almost like a roasted bell pepper, but they are incredibly spicy.*

*If you can't find 'nduja, make your own pork sausage (see p. 238) and add the puree of one roasted bell pepper and the puree of one spicy fresh red chili, using a mortar and pestle. Tropea is also famous for its long red onions, which in the United States are known as Torpedo onions. These onions are sweet enough to be eaten raw. This dish is inspired by Domenico and the ingredients from his hometown.*

¼ cup (60 ml) extra virgin olive oil

1 Torpedo onion or medium red onion, thinly sliced

8 oz (227 g) zucchini, cut in half and thinly sliced on the bias

20 Italian basil leaves, torn

20 parsley sprigs, picked and chopped (about 6 tablespoons)

6 marjoram sprigs, picked and chopped (about 1 tablespoon)

2 tablespoons 'nduja

1 lb (454 g) farfalle or bowtie pasta

3 oz (85 g) pecorino Romano, grated (about ¾ cup)

Bring a large pot of cold water to a boil.

Put the olive oil, onions, and a pinch of salt in a 14-inch (36-cm) sauté pan over medium-low heat. Cook, stirring occasionally, until the onions are translucent.

Add the zucchini, turn the heat to medium, and sauté until they are tender; don't worry if they start to brown slightly. Add the parsley, marjoram, basil, and 'nduja and sizzle the herbs for 1 minute. Turn off the heat and set the pan aside. Taste and adjust the seasoning.

Drop the farfalle into boiling salted water and cook, stirring frequently, until the pasta is al dente. Drain it, reserving ¼ cup (60 ml) cooking water. Transfer the farfalle to the sauté pan. Add ¼ cup pecorino and toss until well combined and creamy, adding cooking water as necessary, and serve immediately with the remaining freshly grated cheese.

# GNOCCHETTI SARDI CON SPECK, ZUCCHINE E RUGHETTA

## GNOCCHETTI SARDI WITH SPECK, ZUCCHINI & ARUGULA

———

*This is a typically northern Italian recipe. Fabio Stocchi, one of the housekeepers at the Academy, taught me how to make this dish.*

*Speck is a deboned dry cured pork shoulder that is then slightly smoked. It has documented origins dating back to the thirteenth century. The smokiness of the speck and the spicy bitterness of the arugula pairs wonderfully with the sweetness of the butter, onions, and zucchini.*

*4 tablespoons (60 g) butter*

*1 medium yellow onion, diced*

*1½ oz (43 g) speck or smoked bacon, cut into ¼-inch (.6-cm) dice*

*2 medium zucchini, cut in half and thinly sliced on the bias*

*3 oz (85 g) arugula, trimmed and cut in half lengthwise if the leaves are long*

*freshly ground black pepper, to taste*

*1 lb (454 g) gnocchetti sardi*

*2 oz (57 g) Grana Padano, grated (about ¾ cup)*

Bring a large pot of cold water to a boil.

Put the butter, onions, and speck in a 14-inch (36-cm) sauté pan over medium heat. Cook, stirring occasionally, until the onions are translucent. A little color is ok.

Add the zucchini and sauté for 4 more minutes. Add half of the arugula, turn off the heat, and stir until the arugula is wilted. Taste and adjust the seasoning.

Drop the gnocchetti sardi into boiling salted water and cook, stirring frequently, until the pasta is al dente. Drain it, reserving ¼ cup (60 ml) cooking water. Transfer the gnocchetti sardi to the sauté pan, turn the heat to medium-high, and toss until well combined, adding cooking water as necessary. Top with remaining arugula and serve immediately with freshly grated Grana.

# GARGANELLI CON PISELLI E PROSCIUTTO
## GARGANELLI WITH ENGLISH PEAS & PROSCIUTTO DI PARMA

———

*This is an RSFP take on two separate dishes: the classic Roman side dish of peas and prosciutto and the primo of garganelli with sausage and peas from Emilia-Romagna.*

*4 tablespoons (60 g) butter*

*½ bunch spring onions, cut in half and thinly sliced (about 1 cup)*

*2 oz (57 g) prosciutto di Parma, cut into ⅛-inch (.3-cm) dice*

*½ cup (118 ml) dry white wine, preferably a Trebbiano*

*2 cups shelled English peas (about 3 lbs [1.4 kg] unshelled)*

*4 oz (118 g) canned whole San Marzano-style tomatoes, pureed with a hand blender or in a food processor*

*1 lb (454 g) garganelli or penne rigate*

*2 oz (57 g) Grana Padano, grated (about ¾ cup)*

Bring a large pot of cold water to a boil.

Put the butter in a 14-inch (36-cm) sauté pan over medium-low heat until it has started to foam. Add the onions and the prosciutto and cook, stirring occasionally, for about 15 minutes. The onion should be translucent and just starting to brown. Add the white wine and let the liquid reduce by three-quarters.

When the water comes to a rolling boil, salt it and cook the peas for 3 minutes. Remove them using a slotted spoon and transfer the peas to the pan. Cook for 3 more minutes, stirring frequently, then add the tomato sauce along with a pinch of salt. Simmer the peas in the tomato puree until they are fully tender. Taste and adjust the seasoning.

Drop the garganelli into boiling salted water and cook, stirring frequently, until the pasta is almost al dente. Drain it 2 minutes before the indicated cooking time, reserving ½ cup (118 ml) cooking water. The pasta will cook for the last few minutes in the sauce and absorb its flavors.

Transfer the garganelli to the sauté pan and turn the heat to medium-high. Simmer the pasta in the sauce for about 2 minutes, adding cooking water as necessary and stirring frequently to avoid sticking. Serve immediately with freshly grated Grana.

# OUVA E FORMAGGIO

# UOVA E FORMAGGIO
## EGG & CHEESE SAUCES

Egg and cheese recipes are the last and perhaps the most challenging set of dry pasta recipes in this book. They really build on the techniques in the previous three sections. These recipes require the cook to work quickly, precisely, and with finesse. They are simple in the beginning and become progressively more complex. While egg and cheese sauces are part of the same section and are made in similar ways, egg recipes deserve some specific attention due to their unique cooking methods (see below for more on egg sauces).

One of the best things about egg and cheese sauces is that they pair so naturally with whole-grain pasta. Whole wheat, kamut, farro, and other types of whole-grain pasta have distinct earthy and nutty flavors. The intensity of these pasta types wonderfully compliments the richness of egg and cheese sauces and creates a nutritious pairing of bold flavors.

The success of an egg and cheese pasta recipe depends almost solely on striking the balance of sauce to pasta. The sauce has to be just right: not too loose and not too dry. The idea is to gauge the exact ratio of ingredients to cooking water to result in a sauce with a perfect creamy consistency; it should adhere to the pasta without weighing it down or overwhelming it.

Egg and cheese sauces are tossed with pasta that is cooked perfectly al dente. As with olio recipes, speed is key: the pasta should be drained and transferred immediately to the pan or bowl to retain as much residual heat as possible. Adding cooking water from the pasta is particularly important to adjust the consistency and creaminess of the sauce. This residual heat and cooking water helps melt the cheese and cook the egg. This is especially true for pasta made with cheese sauces. They must be tossed quickly and served immediately, and eaten hot or very warm before the sauce gets cold and clumps up.

Sauces made with eggs require a precise hand and a watchful eye. They aren't necessarily hard to make, but they are easy to mess up since the dish really comes together in the last few moments of cooking the egg with the pasta in the pan. All eggs, be it chicken eggs, quail eggs, duck eggs, or even fish eggs (such as mullet roe) behave in the same way. When cooked correctly, they thicken to just the right consistency and create a creamy sauce that perfectly coats the pasta. The execution of each recipe requires some finesse and quick thinking to obtain the correct texture and viscosity every time.

With too much heat the eggs can curdle, with too little they remain runny and taste raw. It's a fine line to draw between overdone and underdone, but there is a specific point at which the consistency is just right. The protein in egg whites begins to coagulate—that is to say goes from its liquid form to a thickened mass—at 150°F (65°C), while the protein in egg yolks begins to coagulate at 158°F (70°C). A whole egg, the yolk and the white, sets or coagulates at around 165°F.

If the temperature in the pan is at or over 165°F, the egg is in danger of curdling and turning into scrambled eggs when you toss it with the pasta. Hence, the pasta gets tossed in the pan first to bring the temperature in the pan down, then the egg mixture is added so that it is cooked by the residual heat in the pan, and not by the direct heat of the flame. Once you've tossed the pasta with the egg and a touch of cooking water, let it sit in the pan for about 30 seconds before tossing it again, so that the sauce can absorb the cooking water and continue to thicken up and cook as it sits. Even just a few teaspoons of cooking water will help adjust the thickness of the sauce. If the temperature of the pan is too low and the egg remains runny, place it over low heat, stirring vigorously for a few seconds, moving the pan on and off the heat, until the right consistency is reached—the eggs are cooked but haven't curdled, the sauce is thick and adheres fully to the pasta.

# PACCHERI CACIO E PEPE
## WHOLE-WHEAT PACCHERI WITH PECORINO ROMANO
## & CRACKED BLACK PEPPER

------

*Cacio is the Roman word for cheese. This is one of the four quintessential Roman dishes, along with Carbonara, Gricia, and Amatriciana (although it is technically from Amatrice). Cacio e pepe is traditionally made with fresh tonnarelli (the Roman version of spaghetti alla chitarra), but at the RSFP we like to make this dish with whole-grain pasta, usually made with either farro or whole wheat. The flavor of the whole grain is strong enough to stand up to the sharp and salty sheep's milk cheese.*

*Cacio e pepe is a very simple and quick dish, but it's incredibly delicious and yields truly impressive results. To make this dish really shine, make sure you grind the pepper at the last minute and use real pecorino Romano.*

*1 tablespoon cracked black pepper or coarsely ground black pepper*

*1 tablespoon extra virgin olive oil*

*1 lb (454 g) paccheri or whole-wheat rigatoni*

*3 oz (85 g) pecorino Romano, grated (about ¾ cup), plus more for serving*

Bring a large pot of cold water to a boil.

Crack the pepper or coarsely grind the pepper with a peppermill.

Put the black pepper and olive oil in a large mixing bowl.

Drop the paccheri into boiling salted water and cook, stirring frequently, until the pasta is al dente. Drain the paccheri, reserving 1 cup (237 ml) cooking water. Transfer the pasta to the bowl and toss well to combine. Add about one third of the reserved cooking water and all of the freshly grated pecorino and stir rapidly until a thick creamy sauce has formed. Add more cooking water as necessary, and serve immediately with more freshly grated pecorino.

# PENNE AL BURRO E PARMIGIANO
## PENNE WITH BUTTER & PARMESAN

---

*In the United States, this is known as pasta Alfredo. Pasta Alfredo is originally from Rome, named after the restaurant Alfredo (there were actually two restaurants with this name) that claims to have originated the recipe. Alfredo would serve his legendary pasta to Americans after the war and later to Hollywood movie stars. While the dish may be Roman, it is now far more popular in the United States than it is in Rome.*

*Originally, this recipe does did not contain any cream although many American interpretations use cream (among other things). The butter and Parmigiano are sufficient to create a creamy sauce. Pasta al Burro e Parmigiano contains only three ingredients, so make sure they're of the utmost quality. We like to use whole-grain pasta at the Academy in this dish as a nutritious alternative to white pasta*

| | |
|---|---|
| *1 lb (454 g) whole-grain penne* | Bring a large pot of cold water to a boil. |
| *8 tablespoons (120 g) butter* | Drop the penne into boiling salted water and cook, stirring frequently, until the pasta is al dente. |
| *3 oz (85 g) Parmigiano-Reggiano, grated (about 1 cup), plus more for serving* | While the pasta is cooking, put the butter and ½ cup of the cooking water in a 14-inch (36-cm) sauté pan over low heat, swirling the pan until the butter melts and has emulsified into the water, then turn off the heat. |
| | Drain the penne, reserving ¼ cup (60 ml) cooking water, and transfer the penne to the sauté pan. Add the Parmigiano-Reggiano and toss well until you obtain a creamy sauce, adding cooking water as necessary. Serve immediately with the remaining Parmigiano-Reggiano. |

RESERVED          RESERVED

# PENNE AL GORGONZOLA
## PENNE WITH GORGONZOLA

—————

*Gabriel Soare has worked as the barman of the American Academy for nearly 20 years. He loves pasta* in bianco *(pasta made without tomato sauce, that remains "white"). Penne al Gorgonzola is Gabri's favorite pasta* in bianco. *Whenever we serve this, we make sure to prepare an extra large amount for Gabri's double portion!*

*You can easily turn this into Pasta ai Quattro Formaggi, by replacing the 10 ounces of gorgonzola dolce with the same amount of two other cheeses of your choice, such as taleggio, mascarpone, or pecorino. Those two, along with the gorgonzola piccante and the Grana Padano, comprise the four cheeses of Quattro Formaggi.*

10 oz (283 g) gorgonzola dolce

4 oz (113 g) gorgonzola piccante, crumbled

½ cup (118 ml) half and half

1 lb (454 g) penne

1 teaspoon freshly ground black pepper

2 oz (57 g) Grana Padano, grated (about ¾ cup), optional

Bring a large pot of cold water to a boil.

Combine the half and half and both gorgonzola cheeses in a large metal or Pyrex (not glass) mixing bowl and place the bowl on top of the pasta pot as it comes to a boil, stirring every 5 minutes, so that the gorgonzola starts to melt.

When the water comes to a rolling boil, remove the bowl and drop the penne into boiling salted water and cook, stirring frequently, until the pasta is al dente. Drain the penne and transfer the pasta to the bowl right away. Add the pepper and toss the penne with the cheese sauce until a thick sauce has formed. Serve immediately with freshly grated Grana, if you like.

# FUSILLI ALLA MARCHIGIANA
## FUSILLI WITH SAUSAGE & PECORINO DI FOSSA

---

*This is a dish from Le Marche, a region known for its cooks. I first had it in a trattoria Marchigiana in Rome. It is a simple dish, yet it has an amazing complexity of perfectly balanced subtle flavors in every bite. The garlicky sausage is ground extremely fine and almost resembles a paste as it melts. If you're making your own sausage (which I urge you to try), add ½ of a pounded garlic clove to the mix. The pecorino di Fossa is aged in naturally occurring subterranean holes or man-made pits (fosse) that are typically lined with straw.*

*2 tablespoons extra virgin olive oil*

*10 oz (283 g) sausage (to make your own see p. 238)*

*½ cup (118 ml) dry white wine, like a Verdicchio or Trebbiano Abruzzese*

*½ medium yellow onion, minced*

*1 lb (454 g) fusilli*

*3 oz (85 g) pecorino di Fossa, grated (about ¾ cup), pecorino Toscano, or a pecorino wrapped in a walnut leaf*

*Freshly ground black pepper, to taste*

Bring a large pot of cold water to a boil.

If you are using store-bought sausage, remove the casing. Put the sausage in a food processor and pulse until the sausage falls apart and you obtain a creamy paste.

Put the olive oil, onion, and sausage in a 14-inch (36-cm) sauté pan over medium-low heat. Break up the sausage with a wooden spoon and cook, stirring occasionally, until the sausage is slightly browned and the onion is translucent. Add the white wine and let the liquid reduce by three-quarters. Add 2 cups of cooking water and keep cooking over low heat for 35 minutes, or until the water has evaporated.

Drop the fusilli into boiling salted water and cook, stirring frequently, until the pasta is al dente. Drain it, reserving ½ cup (118 ml) cooking water.

Transfer the fusilli to the pan right away and toss until well combined, adding cooking water as necessary. Top with copious amounts of freshly grated pecorino di Fossa and pepper, and serve immediately.

# RICOTTA

Ricotta, in Italian, literally means re-cooked, or cooked twice. Ricotta is made from whey that is left over during the process of making cheese. The whey is heated in order to curdle any remaining protein that has not coagulated. It is then traditionally left to drain in baskets. Ricotta should be eaten the same day it is made.

Ricotta can be made with virtually any milk. The most commonly found ricotta is made with cow's milk, sheep's milk, or buffalo milk. Cow's milk ricotta is the most readily available in the United States, but it is worth seeking out sheep's milk ricotta or even ricotta made with buffalo or goat's milk.

Sheep's milk ricotta is quintessentially Roman, and we love to use it at the RSFP, in pasta dishes, soufflés, *sformati*, baked, and delicious desserts. Simply served on its own, it's a revelation. Massimo Antonini brings us his sheep's milk ricotta every Thursday while it is still warm. Sheep's milk ricotta has a smaller curd than buffalo and cow's milk ricotta and is a little denser and bolder in taste. In my opinion, it has the most intense flavor of all three because of the wild herbs and grasses that the sheep eat as they graze in the mountains.

Sheep's milk ricotta is particularly good in the spring. As the winter snow melts, shepherds in Italy start to take their sheep into the mountains. This is traditionally known as the *transumanza*, the "crossing of the land," and refers to the biannual migration of flocks or herds from the plains to the mountains, and vice versa. In the spring the sheep move to higher ground in order to escape summer heat; in the fall they come back to the lowlands to stay warm. This tradition has largely been lost, but the sheep's spring migration to the highlands is the last remnant of the *transumanza*. They go from eating hay from the previous year's harvest during the winter months to finally eating fresh wild herbs, grasses, and flowers in the highlands during the spring. This change in diet results in a more nutritious and uniquely flavored ricotta.

# FUSILLI ALLA PECORARA ROMANA

## FUSILLI WITH GUANCIALE, SHEEP'S MILK RICOTTA
## & BLACK PEPPER

———

*One night, after getting home late, I was starving. I started looking around my kitchen to see what I could pull together quickly. I found some ricotta, guanciale, and pecorino in the fridge, threw them together and devoured it in seconds. I was shocked by how good it was and was excited to lay claim to a new instant classic. A few days later, I decided to make it for the workers at the Academy, calling it simply pasta with ricotta, pecorino, and guanciale. Fabio Stocchi, one of the housekeepers, was super excited to see this dish on the menu. He told me there was an actual name for this dish. It's called Pasta alla Pecorara, named after Roman shepherds (pecorari). They would always have pecorino and ricotta among their provisions, and, being Roman, they would naturally always have some guanciale. There went my claim to fame.*

*8 oz (227 g) guanciale or bacon, cut into ½-inch (1.2-cm) dice*

*2 tablespoons extra virgin olive oil*

*12 oz (340 g) sheep's milk ricotta*

*1 teaspoon freshly ground black pepper, plus more for serving*

*1 lb (454 g) fusilli*

*3 oz (85 g) pecorino Romano, grated (about ¾ cup)*

Bring a large pot of cold water to a boil.

Put the guanciale and olive oil in a 14-inch (36-cm) sauté pan over low heat. Cook, stirring occasionally until the guanciale has rendered its fat and has crisped up.

Stir in the ricotta, black pepper, and ¼ cup (60 ml) cooking water, and turn off the heat.

Drop the fusilli into boiling salted water and cook, stirring frequently, until the pasta is al dente. Drain it, reserving ¼ cup (60 ml) cooking water. Transfer the fusilli to the sauté pan and toss well to combine, adding cooking water as necessary. Serve immediately with freshly ground black pepper and grated pecorino.

# PENNE INTEGRALI CON ASPARAGI E RICOTTA

## FARRO PENNE WITH ASPARAGUS, SPRING ONIONS, BASIL & SHEEP'S MILK RICOTTA

*I first tried this combination with Domenico Cortese, a cook at the RSFP for more than two years. I was amazed because the sweetness of the basil went so well with the grassy asparagus. We made this pasta for Alice Waters when she came to visit Rome, and she also instantly fell in love with the way in which the whole-grain pasta brought it all together. We like to dot the ricotta on at the end so you can taste fresh ricotta in each bite, but feel free to mix it in to obtain a creamy sauce.*

⅓ cup (79 ml) extra virgin olive oil

1 bunch spring onions, thinly sliced (about 1 cup)

1 lb (454 g) asparagus, trimmed and cut on the bias, roughly the same size as the penne

20 Italian basil leaves

Freshly ground black pepper, to taste

1 lb (454 g) whole-grain penne

4 oz (113 g) sheep's milk ricotta

2 oz (57 g) Grana Padano, grated (about ¾ cup)

Bring a large pot of cold water to a boil.

Put the olive oil, spring onions, and a pinch of salt in a 14-inch (36-cm) sauté pan over medium-low heat. Cook, stirring occasionally, until the spring onions are translucent.

When the water comes to a rolling boil, salt it and cook the asparagus for just 1 or 2 minutes. Remove it using a slotted spoon and transfer it to the pan.

Sauté the asparagus for 3 minutes, stir in the basil and add ¼ cup (60 ml) cooking water, then turn off the heat. Taste and adjust the seasoning.

Drop the penne into the boiling salted asparagus water. Cook, stirring frequently, until the pasta is al dente. Drain it, reserving ¼ cup (60 ml) cooking water. Transfer the penne to the sauté pan and toss well to combine, adding cooking water as necessary. Dot with ricotta and serve with freshly grated Grana.

# MEZZE MANICHE ALLA CARBONARA
## MEZZE MANICHE WITH EGGS, GUANCIALE, PECORINO & BLACK PEPPER

———

*I like to think of carbonara as the Italian take on a classic American breakfast: it's pasta with bacon and eggs. I love to make this dish before I go skiing because it has all the fundamental elements of a hearty breakfast.*

*There are many stories of the origin of this pasta. My favorite version goes like this: carbonara comes from the Italian word* carbone, *which means coal. When a coal miner would leave town and set up camp for a couple of days at a time, he would take food with him that was nonperishable. Roman coal miners would have brought ingredients like guanciale (cured with spices, like pepper and salt), a hard grating cheese (pecorino Romano), some dry pasta, and a couple of eggs or a chicken that lays eggs while they're set up at camp. The coal miners would make carbonara as a quick yet substantial dish.*

*Another version claims that carbonara is named after the flecks of black pepper on the pasta which resemble* carbone, *or charcoal.*

*This is not a difficult dish to make, but it's an easy dish to mess up because carbonara really comes together in the very last seconds. It can be tricky because you don't want the eggs to curdle and resemble scrambled eggs with pasta. The egg is supposed to form a nice thick creamy sauce that adheres perfectly to the pasta.*

*This is the technique that works best for me: I don't sauté the guanciale until I've dropped the pasta. This allows for the residual heat in the pan to help quickly thicken the egg and cheese without overheating the eggs and risking that they curdle. Have all your ingredients prepared when you drop the pasta so you can pull this together quickly.*

| | |
|---|---|
| *1 lb (454 g) mezze maniche or mezzi rigatoni* | Bring a large pot of cold water to a boil. |
| *8 oz (227 g) guanciale, pancetta, or bacon, cut into ¼-inch (.6-cm) strips* | Drop the mezze maniche into boiling salted water and cook, stirring frequently, until al dente. |
| *1 tablespoon extra virgin olive oil* | Put the guanciale and the olive oil in a 14-inch (36-cm) sauté pan over medium-low heat. Sauté the guanciale, stirring occasionally, until it is browned and crisp. |
| *4 eggs* | |
| *½ tablespoon coarsely ground black pepper, plus more for serving* | Meanwhile, whisk the eggs with ½ cup pecorino and the black pepper. |

*2 oz (85 g) pecorino Romano,
grated (about ½ cup),
plus more for serving*

When the guanciale is nice and crispy, add a 2-ounce (small) ladle of cooking water, and turn off the heat.

When the pasta is al dente, drain it, reserving ¼ cup (60 ml) cooking water. Immediately transfer the pasta to the pan with the guanciale. Toss well to coat the pasta with the guanciale fat.

Add the egg mixture and stir vivaciously until the sauce is thick. Adjust the consistency to your liking using more cooking water, until the sauce adheres fully to the mezze maniche. You may need to turn the heat on for just a couple seconds to help the egg reach the right consistency. Serve immediately with more freshly grated pecorino.

# PENNE ALLA CARBONARA DI ASPARAGI

## PENNE WITH ASPARAGUS, EGGS & MINT

*This is a dish I learned to make from my friend and mentor Cal Peternell, who has been a chef at Chez Panisse for more than 20 years. Many people add cream to classic carbonara to obtain the perfect consistency, but that's cheating by Italian standards. This asparagus carbonara, however, benefits from a touch of cream. Cream allows for more flexibility when cooking carbonara, as it prevents the eggs from curdling too quickly. It rounds out the flavor of the egg and complements the combination of asparagus, spring onion, and mint in this light and delicate creamy sauce.*

½ cup (118 ml) extra virgin olive oil

1 bunch spring onions, thinly sliced (about 1 cup)

6 mint sprigs, picked and chopped (about 2 tablespoons)

1 lb (454 g) asparagus, trimmed and cut on the bias, roughly the same size as the penne

20 parsley sprigs, picked and chopped (about 6 tablespoons)

¼ cup (60 ml) heavy cream

1 lb (454 g) penne

2 eggs

2 egg yolks

3 oz (85 g) Grana Padano, grated (about 1 cup)

1 teaspoon freshly ground black pepper

Bring a large pot of cold water to a boil.

Put the olive oil, spring onions, and a pinch of salt in a 14-inch (36-cm) sauté pan over medium-low heat. Cook, stirring occasionally, until the spring onions are translucent.

When the water comes to a rolling boil, salt it and cook the asparagus for 5 minutes. Remove it using a slotted spoon, reserving water, and transfer the asparagus to the pan. Add the mint and parsley, stir well, and cook for 1 more minute, or until the asparagus is tender. Add the cream and turn off the heat.

Drop the penne into the boiling salted asparagus water. Cook, stirring frequently, until the pasta is al dente.

Meanwhile, whisk the eggs and egg yolks with three-quarters of the Grana and the black pepper.

When the pasta is al dente, drain it, reserving ¼ cup (60 ml) cooking water. Transfer the penne to the sauté pan and toss until well combined, adding cooking water as necessary. Add the egg mix and turn the heat to low. Stir vigorously, over the heat and off the heat, until the sauce is thick. Make sure the egg does not overcook and curdle.

When the sauce has reached the right consistency and it adheres fully to the pasta, serve immediately with the remaining freshly grated Grana.

# LINGUINE CON ZUCCHINE
# E BOTTARGA DI MUGGINE
## LINGUINE WITH ZUCCHINI, BASIL & MULLET BOTTARGA

*Bottarga di muggine is the dried salted pressed roe of a mullet. It is usually a yellowish orange color and has a distinct briny mineral flavor. It is delicious grated or shaved directly onto salads, vegetables, and pastas. In this dish, the roe literally melts when it is hot, creating a creamy sauce, similar to the texture and consistency of the egg emulsification in carbonara.*

*Even though cheese and fish generally don't go well together, this dish highlights the versatility of ricotta salata, which truly complements the creamy bottarga and zucchini here.*

½ cup (118 ml) extra virgin olive oil

1 bunch spring onions, thinly sliced (about 1 cup)

1 teaspoon hot pepper flakes

12 Italian basil leaves, torn

1 lb (454 g) zucchini, cut into ¼-inch (.6-cm) dice, blossoms reserved

3 oz (85 g) mullet bottarga, grated

1 lb (454 g) linguine

2 oz (57 g) ricotta salata, grated on a box grater using the large holes (about 1 cup)

Bring a large pot of cold water to a boil.

Put the olive oil, spring onions, and a pinch of salt in a 14-inch (36-cm) sauté pan over medium-low heat. Cook, stirring occasionally, until the spring onions are translucent. Add the hot pepper and diced zucchini (not the blossoms) along with the basil, and cook for 3 or 4 more minutes, or until the zucchini is tender, then turn off the heat.

Drop the pasta into boiling salted water and cook, stirring frequently, until the pasta is al dente. Drain it, reserving 2 cups (473 ml) cooking water. Transfer the linguine and bottarga to the sauté pan and turn the heat to low. Toss until well combined, adding cooking water as necessary (it will need lots). The bottarga will melt and create a creamy sauce.

Garnish with the zucchini blossoms and freshly grated ricotta salata, and serve immediately.

# PASTA FRESCA

# PASTA FRESCA

## FRESH PASTA

Many of the RSFP interns who come to Rome have never made fresh pasta, and learning this process is integral to our teaching philosophy. Fresh pasta not only demands specific skills, but it also requires commitment and patience. Even if you're not completely satisfied the first time you try making fresh pasta, don't give up. You recognize great pasta dough from touch and feel, and you only gain that understanding from experience.

I recommend making fresh pasta by hand the first few times you try, so you can easily control the dough and get a feel for the correct texture and elasticity. You can definitely make pasta using a standing mixer once you've gotten the hang of it.

Fresh pasta is simply made with flour and a liquid to bind it, so naturally the type of flour is the first thing to take into consideration. Flour is made by milling grains, which contain three main parts: the bran, germ, and endosperm. The endosperm contains most of the carbohydrates, while the bran and germ carry the bulk of nutrients and fiber. The germ also contains nearly half of all the protein.

The protein content of flour is especially important. The amount of protein and its reaction when moistened and kneaded will strongly affect the texture and elasticity of the dough. As you first mix in the water, the gluten protein in flour is activated and the dough becomes elastic. As you continue to knead, the gluten tightens up. The dough then needs to rest so the gluten can relax. Resting makes the dough easier to stretch and shape. This entire process allows the dough to maintain its form during the shaping and cooking process.

Many white flours made from wheat are essentially milled endosperm. At the RSFP we use freshly milled flour that is ground with the germ, so it retains lots of the naturally occurring nutritious fiber and protein. All-purpose flour in the United States works well because it usually has a relatively high protein content. In Italy 00 flour, which has a lower protein content and thus needs to be kneaded for more time, is typically used. At the RSFP we often like to make our fresh pasta with a little semolina for extra chewiness. Seek out high-quality, freshly milled flours. The older the flour (the longer it has sat on a shelf) the drier it becomes and the more liquid it needs to reach the right consistency and texture.

The main difference between flour-water dough and flour-egg dough is the additional fat provided by the egg yolk. Fat acts as a tenderizer but retards the formation of gluten so egg pasta dough must be kneaded longer than flour-water dough in order to develop the gluten necessary to give it its elasticity.

We are calling perfectly cooked fresh pasta "al dente," but it's something quite different from the al dente of dry pasta. Al dente fresh pasta is chewier than its dry counterpart. Perfectly cooked fresh pasta should remain firm yet only slightly yielding to the tooth. It should stretch easily without tearing and be quite springy. Fresh pasta absorbs tons of water as it cooks (far more than dry pasta). It always cooks for the last few minutes in the sauce, absorbing its flavors as it continues to cook in the liquid.

Fresh pasta should be cooked within 24 hours of being made. If you aren't using it immediately, place it on a well-floured baking sheet and cover it with a dish-towel. Fresh pasta freezes well: quick-freeze it first on the baking sheet until it is completely frozen, then put it in an airtight container. It will keep in the freezer for up to three weeks.

Finally, use your judgment. There are numerous factors that will affect the final product: humidity, type of flour, size of eggs, amount of water, etc. You may need to tweak the recipes and experiment a little to find the ingredient ratio that works for you, in the climate in which you live, with the ingredients at hand. Your goal is always to produce a smooth, elastic dough that is "dry" enough to roll out (not excessively moist), but not so dry that it will crack and fall apart.

If you are going to buy fresh pasta, estimate about 5.3 oz (150 g) per person, or 1.3 lb (600 g) for 4 to 6 people.

# IMPASTI
## PASTA DOUGHS

*Fresh pasta, as you'll see, is extremely variable. You can make it with a variety of flours: all-purpose, semolina, whole-wheat, farro, buckwheat, chestnut, kamut... the list goes on. The same goes for the binding liquid: water, eggs, and vegetable purees all work well. You can even add some chopped herbs or a spice like saffron to the dough if you like. Below are the six basic recipes that we use at the RSFP. Each recipe in this book specifies which fresh pasta dough we suggest.*

### FLOUR WATER PASTA
1 lb (454 g) all-purpose flour (00)
7 oz (207 ml) water, almost 1 cup
½ teaspoon salt

### GREEN PASTA
12 oz (342 g) all-purpose flour (00)
4 oz (113 g) semolina
2 eggs
5.3 oz (150 g) pureed greens
(spinach or nettles)
¼ teaspoon salt

### EGG PASTA
12 oz (342 g) all-purpose flour (00)
4 oz (113 g) semolina
3 eggs
3 egg yolks
½ teaspoon salt

### WET EGG PASTA
1 lb (454 g) all-purpose flour (00)
4 eggs
½ teaspoon salt

### WHOLE-GRAIN PASTA
5.32 oz (151 g) all-purpose flour (00)
5.32 oz (151 g) semolina
5.32 oz (151 g) buckwheat or farro flour
4 eggs
½ teaspoon salt

### CHESTNUT PASTA
5.32 oz (151 g) all-purpose flour (00)
5.32 oz (151 g) semolina
5.32 oz (151 g) chestnut flour
4 eggs
½ teaspoon salt

MAKING THE DOUGH

For all pasta doughs, use the following steps:

Weigh the ingredients and sift the flour(s).

Make a well in the flour.

Add the liquid to the well: water, eggs (break the eggs into a small bowl first and whisk them well) or greens puree, along with the salt.

Gradually incorporate the flour into the liquid by pulling the flour from the sides of the well with a fork and mixing it into the liquid using a circular motion.

When the liquid is fully incorporated, keep mixing until the dough forms into a shaggy mass and starts to come together.

Form the dough into a ball.

Use the palm of your hand to knead it. Press and push the dough forward and back across the work surface for 8 to 10 minutes, until it forms into a smooth and elastic ball. It should have a uniform color and spring back to the touch.

Divide the ball into two equal pieces, roll into balls, and wrap them in plastic. Let the balls rest for at least 1 hour to hydrate the dough.

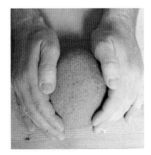

# MAKING FRESH PASTA

Measuring out the ingredients

Making a well in the flour

Dough coming together

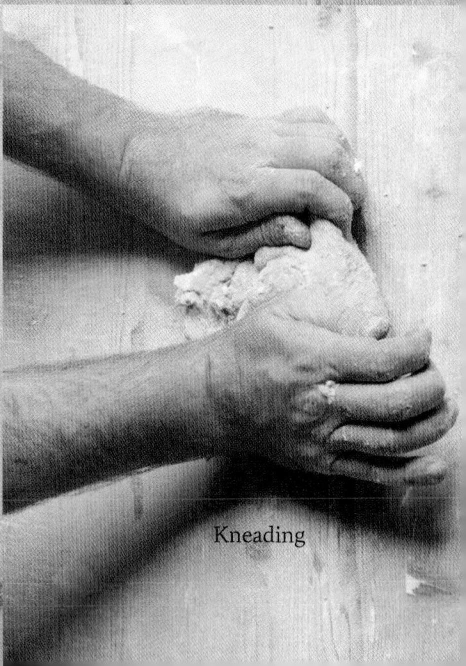

Kneading

154

Adding liquid to the well

Incorporating

Forming the ball

Resting/hydrating the dough

# CAVATELLI

Divide each ball into six equal pieces. Using both hands to roll, start in the middle of the dough and gently extend pressure outwards to form pencil-thin ropes.

Cut the ropes into ½-inch (1.2-cm) lengths.

Press firmly on the top of the cavatelli with the edge of your knife. Using the knife, draw the pasta across the board and pull it towards you exerting moderate pressure.

Place the cavatelli on a floured rimmed baking sheet. Place a clean dishtowel on top of the cavatelli to prevent the pasta from drying.

# CAVATELLI AL POMODORO FRESCO

## CAVATELLI WITH FRESH TOMATO SAUCE

*Cavatelli are dear to me because I learned how to make them during my very first trip to Italy when I lived in Campitello del Mattese in Molise. I love cavatelli because of the unique chewy texture of flour and water pasta (some like to call them the gnocchi of the south). Cavatelli are great for fresh pasta beginners, because like all flour water pasta, they don't require sheeting or laminating, reserved for egg pasta: instant gratification!*

1 batch Flour Water Pasta (see p. 152)

½ cup (118 ml) extra virgin olive oil

4 garlic cloves, smashed

2½ lbs (1.1 kg) ripe San Marzano or Roma tomatoes, made into concassé (see p. 240) or cherry tomatoes cut in half

20 Italian basil leaves

1½ teaspoons hot pepper flakes

2 oz (57 g) Grana Padano or pecorino Romano, grated (about ¾ cup)

Make the Flour Water Pasta (see p. 153).

When the pasta dough has rested, make the cavatelli (see p. 157).

Bring a large pot of cold water to a boil.

Put the olive oil and garlic in a 14-inch (36-cm) sauté pan over medium-low heat. Cook, stirring occasionally, until the garlic is golden, then remove and discard it.

Add the tomatoes, basil, and hot pepper to the pan. Simmer the tomatoes until the sauce is reduced by half, then turn off the heat. Taste and adjust the seasoning.

Drop the cavatelli into boiling salted water and cook, stirring frequently, until the pasta is almost al dente. Drain it, reserving ½ cup (118 ml) cooking water. The pasta will cook for the last few minutes in the sauce and absorb its flavors.

Transfer the cavatelli to the sauce and turn the heat to medium-high. Simmer the pasta in the sauce for about 2 minutes, adding cooking water as necessary and stirring frequently to avoid sticking, until the cavatelli are coated with the sauce. Serve immediately with freshly grated Grana or pecorino.

# CAVATELLI CON COZZE E FAGIOLI FRESCHI

## CAVATELLI WITH FRESH SHELL BEANS,
## MUSSELS & TOMATO

*This is a delicious combination of flavors as well as textures. A wonderful summer variation could include a pinch of saffron added along with the white wine. In the wintertime we always cook dried beans with carrots, celery, and onions, in order to add sweetness to the dried beans. However, fresh beans have such a delicate, naturally sweet flavor that they are delicious on their own, or with a little rosemary and sage to round out their flavor. We also add olive oil right at the beginning to make the beans unctuous and creamy. It's important to let the beans rest for at least an hour once they are cooked so they become firm on the outside and creamy on the inside. I always like to cook a big pot of beans and use them in soups and side dishes throughout the week.*

*1 batch Flour Water Pasta (see p. 152)*

*1 cup fresh shelled borlotti beans (about 1 lb [454 g] unshelled)*

*4 garlic cloves, smashed*

*1 rosemary sprig*

*1 sage sprig*

*½ cup (118 ml) extra virgin olive oil, plus 3 tablespoons*

*1½ lbs (680 g) mussels, scrubbed clean and de-bearded*

*½ cup (118 ml) dry white wine, like a Frascati*

*2 lbs (907 g) Early Girl tomatoes, concassé (see p. 240)*

*1 teaspoon hot pepper flakes*

*15 parsley sprigs, picked and chopped (about 4 tablespoons)*

Prepare the Flour Water Pasta (see p. 153).

Put the fresh beans in a 6-quart (6-liter) saucepot over medium-low heat and cover them with 4 cups water. Add 1 garlic clove, the rosemary, and the sage. Simmer, taking care not to boil the beans and skimming the foam off the surface after 20 minutes. Add 2 tablespoons olive oil and cook for another 40 minutes, or until the beans are tender. Set them aside and let the beans rest for an hour while you make the pasta.

When the pasta dough has rested, make the cavatelli (see p. 157).

Bring a large pot of cold water to a boil.

Put ½ cup olive oil and 3 garlic cloves in a 14-inch (36-cm) sauté pan over medium-low heat. Cook, stirring occasionally, until the garlic is golden, then remove and discard it.

Immediately add the mussels and raise the heat to high. When you start to hear a sizzling sound (after about 30 seconds) add the white wine.

Quickly cover the pan to help steam the mussels open. After about 3 or 4 minutes remove the lid and let the mussels simmer until their shells have opened and they have released their juices. Remove the open mussels from the pan and place them in a bowl. Discard any mussels that have not opened.

Let the mussel juice reduce by half, then add the tomatoes, beans (removing them from the pot with a slotted spoon; don't worry about carrying over some bean liquid), hot pepper, and parsley. Cook for 2 minutes and turn the heat off. Taste and adjust the seasoning.

Drop the cavatelli into boiling salted water and cook, stirring frequently, until the pasta is almost al dente. Drain the cavatelli when they're still quite chewy, reserving 1 cup (237 ml) cooking water. The pasta will cook for the last few minutes in the sauce and absorb its flavors.

Transfer the cavatelli to the sauce and turn the heat to medium-high, add the mussels and simmer the pasta in the sauce for about 2 minutes, adding cooking water as necessary and stirring frequently to avoid sticking, until the cavatelli are coated with the sauce. Serve immediately.

# CAVATELLI ALLA FORAGGINA

## CAVATELLI WITH STINGING NETTLES,
## CHANTERELLE MUSHROOMS & BREADCRUMBS

———

*In the fall, we like to take the new RSFP interns foraging for wild mushrooms and stinging nettles near Viterbo. Every year, Claudia Tonnetti, the head of housekeeping at the Academy, opens up her nearby family home to us. Autumn is a very special time of year, when the new Fellows and scholars are arriving at the Academy. We like to showcase this extremely special dish for the new community. Use gloves when cleaning stinging nettles. Strip the leaves off the stems, discarding only the tough woody stems.*

*1 batch Flour Water Pasta (see p. 152)*

*½ cup (118 ml) extra virgin olive oil*

*2 medium yellow onions, cut into ¼-inch (.6-cm) dice*

*4 thyme sprigs, picked and chopped (about 1 teaspoon)*

*4 garlic cloves, smashed*

*2 lb (907 g) chanterelle mushrooms, carefully cleaned and cut into ½-inch (1.2-cm)-wide wedges (see p. 245)*

*6 oz (170 g) stinging nettles, picked*

*1 cup toasted breadcrumbs (see p. 237)*

*2 oz (57 g) Grana Padano, grated (about ¾ cup)*

Make the Flour Water Pasta (see p. 153).

When the pasta dough has rested, make the cavatelli (see p. 157).

Bring a large pot of cold water to a boil.

Put ¼ cup (60 ml) olive oil, the onions, and a pinch of salt in an 8-inch (20-cm) sauté pan over medium-low heat. Cook until the onions are translucent, add the thyme, then turn off the heat and set the pan aside.

Meanwhile, put ¼ cup (60 ml) olive oil and the garlic in a 14-inch (36-cm) sauté pan over medium heat. When the garlic is golden, remove and discard it. Add the mushrooms and turn the heat to high. Sauté the mushrooms until they are tender and starting to color. Add the stinging nettles to the mushroom pan, season with salt, and sauté for 1 minute. Add the onions and sauté all the ingredients together for 1 minute more, then turn off the heat.

Drop the cavatelli into boiling salted water and cook, stirring frequently, until the pasta is almost al dente.

Drain the cavatelli 2 minutes before they are al dente, reserving 1 cup (237 ml) cooking water. The pasta will cook for the last few minutes in the sauce and absorb its flavors.

Transfer the cavatelli to the pan and turn the heat to medium-high. Simmer the pasta in the sauce for about 2 minutes, adding cooking water as necessary and stirring frequently to avoid sticking. Top with breadcrumbs and serve immediately with freshly grated Grana.

# MACCHERONI AI FERRI

Divide each ball into six equal pieces. Using both hands to roll, start
in the middle of the dough and gently extend pressure outward to form
pencil-thin ropes.

Cut the ropes into 1-inch (2.5-cm) lengths.

Wrap the dough around the metal rod. Roll the rod on a floured surface.
Using both hands, start in the middle and gently extend pressure outwards
to form 5-inch-long maccheroni. Carefully slide the pasta off the rod
and place it on a floured sheet tray or rimmed baking sheet. Place a clean
dishtowel on top of the maccheroni to prevent the pasta from drying.

# MACCHERONI AI FERRI CON SUGO DELLA DOMENICA

## HAND-ROLLED FUSILLI PASTA WITH SUNDAY RAGU

*This classic southern Italian dish is often prepared on Sundays or for special occasions, when traditionally the meat is slowly simmered all morning before a large family lunch. As with spaghetti and meatballs, the sauce is traditionally used to dress the pasta for the* primo *and the meat itself is served as the* secondo. *We like to use shoulder cuts for this sauce because it has the proper muscle-to-fat ratio; the meat becomes meltingly tender as it cooks and falls apart in the tomato sauce.*

*1 batch Flour Water Pasta (see p. 152)*

*¼ cup (60 ml) extra virgin olive oil*

*1 lb (454 g) pork shoulder, cut into 1-inch (2.5-cm) cubes*

*1 lb (454 g) beef chuck, cut into 1-inch (2.5-cm) cubes*

*1 medium yellow onion, cut into ½-inch (1.2-cm) dice*

*1 cup (237 ml) red wine, like a Montepulciano*

*44 oz (1.25 kg) canned whole San Marzano-style tomatoes, pureed with a hand blender or in a food processor*

*1 teaspoon hot pepper flakes*

*15 Italian basil leaves*

*2 oz (57 g) pecorino Romano, grated (about ½ cup)*

Prepare the Flour Water Pasta (see p. 153).

Put the olive oil and the meat in a 14-inch (36-cm) high-sided sauté pan over medium heat. Sear the meat for a few minutes without stirring.

Once the meat has browned slightly and a crust has formed, stir it every so often and continue browning it for 10 to 15 minutes. Add the onion and finish browning the meat on all sides while the onion cooks. When the onion is translucent, add the red wine and reduce the liquid by half.

Add the tomato and hot pepper, and turn the heat to low. When the sauce comes to a simmer, cover it with a lid and cook for two and a half hours, or until the meat is tender, adding water if the sauce level is more than halfway below the meat. Make sure the meat is at least halfway submerged in liquid at all times. After 1 hour, taste and adjusting the seasoning.

When the pasta dough has rested, make the maccheroni ai ferri (see p. 165).

When the meat is meltingly tender, turn off the heat, remove the pieces of meat, and transfer them to a dish. The meat can then be eaten as a secondo. Keep a few smaller pieces of meat in the sauce, if you like.

Bring a large pot of cold water to a boil.

Drop the maccheroni ai ferri into boiling salted water and cook, stirring frequently, until the pasta is almost al dente. Drain the maccheroni 2 minutes before they are al dente, reserving 1 cup (237 ml) cooking water. The pasta will cook for the last few minutes in the sauce and absorb its flavors.

Transfer the pasta to the tomato sauce and add the basil. Turn the heat to medium-high and simmer the pasta in the sauce for about 2 minutes, adding cooking water as necessary and stirring frequently to avoid sticking. Serve immediately with freshly grated pecorino.

# SHEETING & LAMINATING

On a well-floured surface, flatten the dough balls into a rectangular shape using a rolling pin until the dough is roughly ¼-inch (.5-cm) thick.

Open the rollers of the pasta machine to the widest setting. Run the dough through the machine 3 times, each time adjusting the setting of the rollers to the next thinnest setting, until the dough is about half of its initial thickness. Make sure to keep the dough parallel with the edges of the rollers and use flour as necessary to prevent sticking.

Fold the ends of the dough into the center, making sure the width of the dough does not exceed the width of the rollers. Repeat the above process in its entirety 2 additional times.

Cut the sheets into 12-inch (30-cm) lengths. You should get about eight 12-inch (30-cm)-long sheets per batch of dough. Put the sheets on a floured surface or baking sheet and dust with flour in between each sheet so they don't stick together. Place a clean dishtowel on top of sheets to prevent the dough from drying.

# FAZZOLETTI

Sheet and laminate the dough (see p. 169).

Stack 4 sheets of dough, one on top of the other, making sure to dust in between each sheet with flour so the sheets don't stick together. Cut each sheet into 2" x 3" (5 x 8 cm) rectangles.

Place the stacked fazzoletti on a floured sheet tray or rimmed baking sheet. Place a clean dishtowel on top of fazzoletti to prevent the pasta from drying.

Repeat the process with the remaining pasta sheets.

# FAZZOLETTI CON PESTO AI PISTACCHI
## FAZZOLETTI WITH PISTACHIO PESTO

*Giovanni Guerrera, the sous chef at the RSFP for one year, first tasted this on vacation with his family in Sicily. We adapted the recipe and it has become an Academy favorite among the Fellows. This Sicilian-influenced dish combines two of the island's signature products: pistachios and oranges. The orange zest perfectly complements the flavor of the toasted pistachios, creating a fruity and nutty pesto.*

*Fazzoletto is the Italian word for tissue. These large floppy rectangles are easy to make and fun to eat. You can use whole-grain flour here as well.*

| | |
|---|---|
| *1 batch Egg Pasta (see p. 152)* | Prepare the Egg Pasta (see p. 153). |
| *3½ oz (100 g) pistachios* | Preheat the oven to 300°F (150°C). |
| *½ cup (118 ml) extra virgin olive oil* | Spread the pistachios evenly on a sheet pan and toast for 8 minutes, or until the skins begin to split. While the nuts are still warm, place them inside a clean tea towel. Gather the towel into a secure bundle and roll the nuts in a circular motion to loosen and remove some of the skins, and with them any extra bitterness. Lift the nuts out of the towel, shaking off the skins. |
| *15 Italian basil leaves* | |
| *15 parsley sprigs, picked (about ¼ cup parsley leaves)* | |
| *2 tablespoons pecorino Romano, plus more to taste* | |
| *1 tablespoon Grana Padano, plus more to taste* | Put the pistachios, olive oil, basil, and parsley in a hand blender or food processor and blend until smooth. Stir in the pecorino and Grana. Set the pesto aside for 1 hour to develop its flavor. |
| *½ teaspoon lemon juice, or more to taste* | |
| *The zest of 1 orange* | When the pasta dough has rested, make the fazzoletti (see p. 171). |
| | Bring a large pot of cold water to a boil. |
| | After an hour add the lemon juice to the pesto, then taste and adjust the seasoning adding more lemon juice, salt, Grana or pecorino. |

Drop the fazzoletti into boiling salted water and cook, stirring frequently, until the pasta is al dente.

Drain the fazzoletti, reserving ½ cup (118 ml) cooking water. Transfer the pasta and pesto to a large mixing bowl and toss until well combined, adding cooking water as necessary. Grate the orange zest directly over the bowl and serve immediately.

# CORZETTI

A corzetti stamp comes with two pieces, a top piece and a bottom one. The bottom is used in two distinct ways: the bottom of the bottom piece is hollow and has a cookie-cutter-like function, while the top of the bottom piece is used to imprint a design on one side of the corzetti.

Sheet and laminate the dough (see p. 169).

Use the bottom (of the bottom half) of the corzetti stamp to cut the dough: press firmly into each sheet to cut out disks of pasta.

Insert each pasta disk into the corzetti stamp and press down firmly to imprint the design of the corzetti on both sides (there is usually a different design on each side of the stamp).

Put the corzetti on a floured sheet tray or rimmed baking sheet. Place a clean dishtowel on top of the corzetti to prevent the pasta from drying.

Use the remaining scraps of pasta in soups or for Pasta e Ceci or Pasta e Fagioli.

# CORZETTI CON PESTO ALLA MAGGIORANA

## CORZETTI WITH MARJORAM PESTO

*The name Corzetti derives from the silver coins, called crosazzi, that were used during the Republic of Genoa in the thirteenth and fourteenth centuries Decorated with a Figure 8, to symbolize the infinity of the Republic, the coins were pressed directly onto the fresh pasta dough, imprinting the pasta, too, with the image.*

*Corzetti are traditionally dressed with a marjoram sauce made with pine nuts and butter, but we like to make them with a marjoram pesto with walnuts and olive oil. The whole-wheat flour matches well with the beautiful floral perfume of the marjoram.*

*I prefer to use a mortar and pestle, as I do when I make Pesto alla Genovese, but feel free to use a hand blender.*

1 batch Whole-grain Pasta (see p. 152)

3 oz (85 g) walnuts

½ garlic clove

¾ cup (177 ml) extra virgin olive oil, plus 3 to 4 tablespoons

1 bunch marjoram, picked (about ¼ cup marjoram leaves)

1 small bunch parsley, picked and chopped (about 1 cup)

1 oz (28 g) pecorino Toscano or Fiore Sardo, grated (about ¼ cup)

1 oz (28 g) Grana Padano, grated (about ¼ cup)

Prepare the Whole-grain Pasta (see p. 153).

Preheat the oven to 300°F (150°C).

Spread the walnuts evenly on a baking sheet and toast for 10 minutes, or until the skins begin to split and the nuts are fragrant. While the nuts are still warm, place them inside a clean tea towel. Gather the towel into a secure bundle and roll the nuts in a circular motion to loosen and remove some of the skins, and with them any extra bitterness. Lift the nuts out of the towel, leaving behind the skins.

Pound the walnuts in a mortar and pestle until the mixture has a chunky peanut butter-like consistency. Remove and set the walnuts aside in a small bowl.

In the same mortar, pound the garlic with a pinch of salt into a smooth paste, then set it aside and cover it with 1 tablespoon olive oil so that the garlic does not oxidize.

Pound the marjoram with a pinch of salt. As the marjoram breaks down, start using a circular smearing motion to turn the leaves into a paste. Set the marjoram aside and add 1 or 2 tablespoons olive oil to the marjoram, so that it doesn't turn brown. Repeat the same process with the parsley.

In a medium bowl, combine all of the pounded herbs, walnuts, some of the garlic, ¾ cup olive oil, the pecorino, and ¼ cup Grana, and mix until the pesto is smooth. Set it aside in the fridge for 1 hour to allow the flavors to develop. After an hour, taste and adjust the seasoning, adding more garlic, cheese, salt, or olive oil as necessary.

When the pasta dough has rested, make the corzetti (see p. 175).

Bring a large pot of cold water to a boil.

Drop the corzetti into boiling salted water and cook, stirring frequently, until they are al dente. Drain the pasta, reserving ½ cup (118 ml) cooking water. Transfer the pasta and pesto to a large mixing bowl and toss until well combined, adding cooking water as necessary. Serve immediately with freshly grated Grana.

# CUTTING LONG PASTA

Sheet and laminate the dough (see p. 169).

Dust the sheets with flour. Roll each sheet onto itself lengthwise as if you were rolling a scroll.

Depending on the pasta you are making, cut the roll into the appropriate width (see photo below, left to right):

Tagliolini ⅛-inch (.3-cm) thick;
Tagliatelle ¼-inch (.6-cm) thick;
Fettuccine ⅓-inch (.8-cm) thick;
Pappardelle ¾-inch (1.9-cm) thick;

Carefully unfold the roll and separate the pasta ribbons.

Place the ribbons of pasta on a floured rimmed baking sheet. Place a clean dishtowel on top of the noodles to prevent the pasta from drying.

# FETTUCCINE AL RAGÙ
## FETTUCCINE WITH SOUTHERN-STYLE RAGÙ

*When we think of ragù in the United States, we envision a hybrid between a southern Italian ragù and a ragù Bolognese, from the North. The American notion of ragù has lots of tomato sauce, like the southern Italian version, yet it also contains the carrot, celery, and onions of a ragù Bolognese.*

*Marco Cassani, one of our gardeners, was celebrating his birthday, and I told him I would make him whatever he wanted for lunch. He requested fettuccine al ragù. I went through the painstaking process of making the fettuccine by hand and the ragù—or what I thought was the ragù—only to find out that my ragù was in fact a ragù Bolognese, rich with milk and broth but without tomato; and what he wanted was a tomato-based ragù, as it is prepared in the South. This is the ragù I should have made.*

| | |
|---|---|
| *1 batch Egg Pasta (see p. 152)* | Prepare the Egg Pasta (see p. 153). |
| *¼ cup (60 ml) extra virgin olive oil* | Put the olive oil, garlic, and ground meat in a 14-inch (36-cm) high-sided sauté pan over medium-high heat. Add all the meat at once, breaking it up with a wooden spoon and stirring frequently as you sauté. Season with salt and cook for about 15 minutes, or until the meat starts to brown (don't worry about browning it evenly). The meat will weep its juices and then simmer in its own liquid. The juices will start to reduce and will eventually create a *fondo* or base, on the bottom of the pan. The idea is to have a gentle browning on the meat before adding the tomato sauce. When the garlic is golden, discard it. |
| *3 garlic cloves, smashed* | |
| *18 oz (510 g) ground beef* | |
| *12 oz (340 g) ground pork* | |
| *1 cup (237 ml) red wine, like a Nero d'Avola* | |
| *44 oz (1.25 kg) canned San Marzano-style tomatoes, pureed with a hand blender or in a food processor* | Deglaze the meat *fondo* with red wine and cook until the liquid has reduced by two-thirds. |
| *1 teaspoon hot pepper flakes* | Stir in the tomato puree, adjust the heat to low, and cover the pan with a lid. Let the ragù simmer slowly for at least 1 hour. If the liquid starts to reduce excessively and the meat is exposed, add water so that the meat remains |
| *2 oz Grana Padano, grated (about ¾ cup)* | |

submerged in liquid at all times. After 1 hour, taste and adjust the seasoning and continue cooking until the meat is completely tender.

When the pasta dough has rested, make the fettuccine (see p. 179).

Bring a large pot of cold water to a boil.

Drop the fettuccine into boiling salted water and cook, stirring frequently, until the pasta is almost al dente. The pasta will cook for the last few minutes in the sauce and absorb its flavors. Drain the fettucine 2 minutes before they are al dente, reserving 1½ cups (355 ml) of cooking water. Transfer the fettuccine to the sauce and turn the heat to medium-high. Simmer the pasta in the sauce for about 2 minutes, adding cooking water as necessary and stirring frequently to avoid sticking, until the pasta is coated with the sauce. Serve immediately with freshly grated Grana.

# FETTUCCINE VERDI COI CARCIOFI

## STINGING NETTLE FETTUCCINE WITH ARTICHOKES, GREEN GARLIC & MENTUCCIA

*To me the absolute best pasta to use for Pasta coi Carciofi is a fresh green egg pasta. This stunning version is what we like to make for vegetarian night on Wednesdays, because the pureed greens in the Fettuccine Verdi add an extra nutritious vegetable to the meal.*

*The marriage of wild mint (mentuccia) and artichokes takes the vegetable to a higher level. If you can't get mentuccia, substitute a combination of fresh mint and fresh oregano.*

*I like to stew the artichokes with lots of olive oil and a little bit of the lemon water used for cleaning the artichokes. I prefer not to use wine with artichokes because it interferes with the unique flavor of the chemical in the artichoke called Cynar. Using the artichoke lemon water allows you to have the acidity that wine usually provides in cooking.*

*1 batch Green Pasta (see p. 152)*

Prepare the Green Pasta (see p. 153).

*1 lemon*

*½ cup (118 ml) extra virgin olive oil*

*½ bunch green garlic, green part removed and white part cut into ¼-inch dice (about 1 cup)*

Put the olive oil and green garlic in a 14-inch (36-cm) sauté pan over medium-low heat. Cook, stirring occasionally, until the garlic is just golden. Add the artichokes, mentuccia, and 2 cups of the lemon water and a pinch of salt, and cover the pan with a lid. Stew the artichokes for 20 minutes, or until they are tender.

*4 large globe artichokes, cleaned and sliced (see p. 245)*

Bring a large pot of cold water to a boil.

*2 sprigs mentuccia (about 1 teaspoon), picked and chopped or 2 sprigs mint and 1 sprig oregano, picked and chopped (about 2 teaspoons)*

When the pasta dough has rested, make the fettuccine (see p. 179).

Drop the fettuccine into boiling salted water and cook, stirring frequently, until the pasta is almost al dente.

*3 oz (85 g) Grana Padano, grated (about 1 cup)*

Drain the fettucine 2 minutes before they are al dente, reserving ½ cup (118 ml) cooking water. The pasta will cook for the last few minutes in the sauce and absorb its flavors.

Transfer the fettuccine to the pan, and turn the heat to medium-high. Simmer the pasta in the sauce for about 1 minute, stirring frequently to avoid sticking and adding cooking water as necessary, until the fettuccine are coated with the sauce. Serve immediately with freshly grated Grana.

# FETTUCCINE ALLA PAPALINA
## FETTUCCINE WITH HAM, PEAS, EGGS & PARMESAN

———

*These fettucine were first prepared for a cardinal at a Roman trattoria. The name of the dish was changed to* papalina *after Pope Pio XII tasted it and loved it.*

*This dish is uncharacteristic of Roman food, because it contains butter and cream, two ingredients traditionally used in northern Italian cooking. Yet the richness of this dish is characteristic of papal cuisine, famous for its abundant and decadent food symbolizing the wealth and power of the Vatican.*

*Fettuccine alla Papalina is similar to carbonara in that the egg added at the end needs to cook only slightly without curdling. Alternate moving the pan on and off the flame to reach the right consistency and avoid egg curdling.*

| | |
|---|---|
| *1 batch Egg Pasta (see p. 152)* | Prepare the Egg Pasta (see p. 153). |
| *2 tablespoons (30 g) butter* | When the pasta dough has rested, make the fettuccine (see p. 179). |
| *3 oz (85 g) prosciutto di Parma, cut into ¼-inch (.6-cm) cubes* | Bring a large pot of cold water to a boil. |
| *2 spring onions, thinly sliced on the bias* | Put the butter in a 14-inch (36-cm) sauté pan over medium heat and cook until it is foamy. Add the prosciutto and the spring onions and cook until the onions are translucent. Stir in the heavy cream and turn off the heat. |
| *¼ cup (60 ml) heavy cream* | |
| *1 egg* | |
| *2 egg yolks* | In a small bowl, whisk the eggs and egg yolks with ½ cup Grana and season abundantly with black pepper. |
| *2 oz (57 g) Grana Padano, grated (about ¾ cup)* | |
| *Freshly ground black pepper, to taste* | Drop the peas into boiling salted water and add the fettuccine after 4 minutes. Cook, stirring frequently, until the pasta is almost al dente. |
| *2 cups shelled peas (about 3 lbs [1.4 kg] unshelled)* | Drain the fettuccine 2 minutes before they are al dente, reserving ¼ cup (60 ml) cooking water. Transfer the fettuccine and peas to the sauté pan and toss until well combined. |

Add the egg mix and turn the heat to low. Stir vigorously, while moving the pan on and off the heat, adding cooking water as necessary, until the sauce is thick and the pasta is well coated. Make sure the egg does not overcook and curdle. When the sauce reaches the right consistency, serve immediately with the remaining freshly grated Grana.

# TAGLIATELLE AL RAGÙ BOLOGNESE
## TAGLIATELLE WITH RAGÙ BOLOGNESE

---

*Ragù Bolognese is taken so seriously in Bologna that, in 1982, an official recipe was sanctioned by the city's Chamber of Commerce. The idea is to barely stain the Bolognese with a touch of tomato sauce or tomato conserva, not to turn the sauce red. In the winter, instead of celery and white wine, I like to use celery root and red wine (like a Sangiovese); the celery root adds a nice spice quality to the sauce. In the spring I always like to make Bolognese with peas, white wine, and celery.*

*1 batch Egg Pasta (see p. 152)*

*3 tablespoons (45 g) butter*

*1 tablespoon extra virgin olive oil*

*1 large yellow onion, cut into ¼-inch (.6-cm) dice*

*1 medium carrot, cut into ¼-inch (.6-cm) dice*

*3 celery stalks, cut into ¼-inch (.6-cm) dice*

*1 oz (28 g) prosciutto di Parma, cut into ¼-inch (.6-cm) dice*

*9 oz (255 g) beef chuck, ground*

*9 oz (255 g) pork shoulder, ground*

*3 oz (85 g) fresh pork belly, ground*

*2 oz (57 g) tomato puree*

*1 cup (237 ml) dry white wine, like a Trebbiano*

Put the butter in a 14-inch (36-cm) high-sided pan over medium heat. When the butter has melted, add the onion, carrot, celery, prosciutto, and a pinch of salt and cook, stirring occasionally, until the onions are translucent and the carrot and celery are starting to color.

Add the beef and cook until it has wept its juices and has started to brown, breaking it up with a wooden spoon and stirring frequently as you sauté. Remove the meat and vegetables from the pan and set them aside.

Put 1 tablespoon olive oil, the ground pork, and the pork belly in the pan over medium heat. Cook, stirring occasionally, until the meat has wept its juices and has started to brown.

Return the browned beef and vegetables to the pan. Add the tomato puree and cook for 3 minutes.

Deglaze the pan with the white wine and let the liquid reduce by two-thirds.

Add the broth and turn the heat to low. Bring to a simmer, and cover with a lid. Simmer the sauce slowly for about 2 hours.

*3 cups (710 ml) beef or chicken broth (to make your own see pp. 234–35)*

*2 cups (473 ml) whole milk*

*Freshly ground black pepper, to taste*

*Freshly ground nutmeg, to taste*

*20 parsley sprigs, picked and chopped (about 6 tablespoons)*

*2 oz (57 g) Parmigiano-Reggiano, grated (about ¾ cup)*

After 1 hour, add half of the milk. Keep adding it in increments until you've used up all the milk, making sure that the meat is at least halfway submerged in liquid at all times for the rest of the cooking time.

Prepare the Egg Pasta (see p. 153).

When the pasta dough has rested, make the tagliatelle (see p. 179).

Bring a large pot of cold water to a boil.

When the ragù is cooked, taste and adjust the seasoning with salt, pepper, and a touch of nutmeg.

Drop the tagliatelle into boiling salted water and cook, stirring frequently, until the pasta is almost al dente. Drain the tagliatelle 2 minutes before they are al dente, reserving 1 cup (237 ml) cooking water. The pasta will cook for the last few minutes in the sauce and absorb its flavors.

Transfer the pasta to the ragu Bolognese. Add the parsley and turn the heat to medium-high. Simmer the pasta in the sauce for about 2 minutes, adding cooking water as necessary and stirring frequently to avoid sticking. Serve with freshly grated Parmigiano.

# TAGLIATELLE AI FUNGHI PORCINI
## TAGLIATELLE WITH PORCINI MUSHROOMS & NEPITELLA

———

*Nepitella is a wild herb (known as lesser calamint) that typically grows in and around the same places where porcini are found. It is the herb of choice to accompany porcini in Italy. If you can't find nepitella in the United States, use a combination of mint, parsley, and sage. In Italy, porcini are traditionally sautéed in olive oil only. However, I like to use a combination of olive oil with a touch of butter, which adds a subtle sweetness to the dish. This is a trick that I learned from Phillip Deadlow, a friend of mine who was a cook at the Downstairs at Chez Panisse for more than 20 years. I use only salt and black pepper to season mushrooms; hot pepper covers the flavor of the delicate mushrooms.*

*1 batch Egg Pasta (see p. 152)*

Prepare the Egg Pasta (see p. 153).

*¼ cup (60 ml) extra virgin olive oil*

Put the olive oil and butter in a 14-inch (36-cm) sauté pan over medium-high heat.

*2 tablespoons (30 g) butter*

*4 garlic cloves, smashed*

*2 lbs (907 g) porcini mushrooms, cleaned and sliced ¼-inch (.6 cm) thick (see p. 245)*

When the butter begins to foam, add the garlic and mushrooms. Sauté until the mushrooms start to brown slightly. Turn the heat to low and add the nepitella. Continue cooking for about 3 more minutes, until the mushrooms are completely tender. Season with salt and pepper only once the mushrooms are fully cooked to maintain a firm texture. Turn off the heat and set the pan aside.

*4 sprigs nepitella (or 3 mint sprigs, 10 parsley sprigs, and 1 sage leaf) picked and chopped (about 4 tablespoons)*

*Freshly ground black pepper, to taste*

When the pasta dough has rested, make the tagliatelle (see p. 179).

Bring a large pot of cold water to a boil.

*2 oz (57 g) Grana Padano, grated (about ¾ cup)*

Drop the tagliatelle into boiling salted water and cook, stirring frequently, until the pasta is almost al dente. Drain the tagliatelle 2 minutes before they are al dente, reserving 1 cup (237 ml) of cooking water. The pasta will cook for the last few minutes in the sauce and absorb its flavors.

Transfer the tagliatelle to the pan and turn the heat to
medium-high. Simmer the pasta in the sauce for about
2 minutes, adding cooking water as necessary and
stirring frequently to avoid sticking, until the tagliatelle
are coated with the sauce. Serve immediately with
freshly grated Grana.

# PIZZOCCHERI ALLA VALTELLINESE

## BUCKWHEAT PASTA WITH CABBAGE, POTATOES & BITTO CHEESE

*I first had this pasta at a small osteria in the Valtellina, a town known for il Bitto del Bitto della Valtellina, a cheese that is unique because it is made from ⅘ cow's milk and ⅕ goat's milk, which adds just a hint of sharpness. This dish is traditionally made with pizzoccheri, a buckwheat pasta similar to tagliatelle but cut into 3-inch (7.5-cm) lengths.*

*In our kitchen we prepare tester dishes in advance in order to make the proper adjustments before the final meal is served. One of the elements that we analyze is the edibility of the dish—we ask, "How does it eat?" To answer that question, we think about seasoning, texture, and balance. This dish eats fantastically. It has a variety of textures from the pasta, cabbage, and potatoes, and the copious amount of just-melted Bitto cheese ties it all together. I am always amazed at how six distinct flavors can be tasted in every bite. This is quite a hearty dish; this recipe can serve up to eight hungry people.*

1 batch Whole-grain Pasta made with buckwheat flour (see p. 152)

4 tablespoons (60 g) butter

2 medium yellow onions, cut into ½-inch (1.2-cm) dice

10 thyme sprigs, picked and chopped (about 2 teaspoons)

2 teaspoons freshly ground black pepper

¼ cup (60 ml) dry white wine, preferably a Chardonnay or Roero Arneis

2 medium Yukon Gold potatoes, peeled and cut into ¼-inch (.6-cm) cubes

Prepare the Whole-grain Pasta (see p. 153).

When the pasta dough has rested, make the pizzocheri: simply cut the pasta into ¼-inch widths (like tagliatelle, see p. 179), but this time cut the tagliatelle into thirds across the width of the pasta sheet (not the length). Place the pizzocherri on a floured sheet tray or rimmed baking sheet. Place a clean dishtowel on top of the pizzocherri to prevent the pasta from drying.

Bring a large pot of cold water to a boil.

Put the butter in a 14-inch (36-cm) sauté pan over medium-low heat. When the butter has melted, add the onions and a pinch of salt, and cook, stirring occasionally, until the onions are translucent. Add the pepper and thyme, cook for 30 more seconds, then add the white wine. Let the liquid reduce by two-thirds and turn off the heat. Taste and adjust the seasoning.

*1 small head savoy cabbage, cut into 1-inch (2.5-cm) dice (about 8 cups)*

*4 oz (113 g) Bitto or Fontina cheese, grated on a box grater using the large holes (about 2 cups)*

When the water comes to a rolling boil, salt it and add the potatoes and cabbage. Cook for 8 to 12 minutes, or until the potatoes are tender. Using a slotted spoon, transfer the potatoes and cabbage to the onions and turn the heat to medium-high. Mix well to combine and turn off the heat.

Drop the pizzoccheri into boiling salted water and cook, stirring frequently, until the pasta is al dente. Drain it and transfer the pizzoccheri to the sauté pan. Toss until well combined, then add the Bitto, tossing some more until the cheese is just starting to melt. Serve immediately.

# TAGLIOLINI CON RADICCHIO, PANCETTA E MASCARPONE

## TAGLIOLINI WITH RADICCHIO, PANCETTA & MASCARPONE

*There are several varietals of radicchio named after town in the Veneto region. For this pasta I prefer to use the long vareiety of radicchio known as radicchio di Treviso because the firm texture of its ribs is more suited to cooking. Castel Franco and Chioggia (the round kind, simply called radicchio in the United States) are better suited to salads.*

*1 batch Egg Pasta (see p. 152)*

*2 tablespoons extra virgin olive oil*

*8 oz (227 g) bacon or smoked pancetta, cut into ¼-inch (.6-cm) strips*

*1 lb (454 g) Treviso radicchio, cut into ¼-inch (.6-cm) strips*

*1 cup (237 ml) red wine, like a Rosso della Valpolicella*

*2 tablespoons mascarpone*

*Freshly ground black pepper, to taste*

*10 parsley sprigs, picked and chopped (about 3 tablespoons)*

*2 oz (57 g) Grana Padano, grated (about ¾ cup), optional*

Prepare the Egg Pasta (see p. 153).

When the pasta dough has rested, make the tagliolini (see p. 179).

Bring a large pot of cold water to a boil.

Put the olive oil and pancetta in a 14-inch (36-cm) sauté pan over medium-high heat.

When the pancetta has just started to brown, add the radicchio and sauté, stirring occasionally, until it is tender. Add the red wine and reduce the liquid by two-thirds.

Add the mascarpone and season with salt and lots of freshly ground black pepper. Turn off the heat and set the pan aside. Taste and adjust the seasoning.

Drop the tagliolini into boiling salted water and cook, stirring frequently, until the pasta is almost al dente. (The pasta will cook for the last few minutes in the sauce and absorb its flavors.) Drain the tagliolini 2 minutes before they are al dente, reserving ¼ cup (59 ml) cooking water. Transfer the pasta to the pan and turn the heat to medium-high. Simmer the tagliolini in the sauce for about 1 minute, adding cooking water as necessary and stirring frequently to avoid sticking, until the tagliolini are coated with the sauce. Garnish with parsley and serve immediately with freshly grated Grana, if you like.

# PAPPARDELLE CON CACCIAGIONE E PISELLI

## PAPPARDELLE WITH TURKEY RAGÙ & ENGLISH PEAS

---

*This ragù can be prepared with any game, such as duck, goose, pheasant, or even rabbit.
I like to use celery root instead of celery, which adds a nice spicy quality to the ragu that
is wonderful in the winter. The boiled peas and chopped herbs really brighten the dish.*

| | |
|---|---|
| *1 batch Egg Pasta (see p. 152)* | Prepare the Egg Pasta (see p. 153). |
| *½ cup dried porcini mushrooms* | Pour 1 cup (237 ml) of boiling water over the porcini and steep them for 10 minutes. Remove the porcini from the water and chop them, reserving the liquid. Carefully pour the porcini liquid into another cup and reserve the porcini "tea," discarding the sediment left from steeping. |
| *¼ cup (60 ml) extra virgin olive oil* | |
| *1 medium yellow onion, cut into ¼-inch (.6-cm) dice* | |
| *½ celery root, cut into ¼-inch (.6-cm) dice* | Preheat the oven to 300°F (150°C). |
| *2 whole turkey legs (about 5 lbs [2.27 kg])* | Remove the skin from the turkey legs and chop it up. |
| *1 cup (237 ml) dry white wine, like a Verdicchio di Matelica* | Put the olive oil, onion, celery, turkey skin, and chopped porcini in a 14-inch (36-cm) high-sided sauté pan over medium heat. Cook, stirring occasionally, until the onion is translucent. |
| *2 cups (473 ml) chicken broth (see p. 234)* | |
| *2 sage sprigs* | Add the turkey legs, turn the heat to medium-low, and brown the meat on all sides. Add the white wine and let the liquid reduce by half. |
| *1 cup shelled English peas (about 1 lb [454 g] unshelled)* | |
| *4 tablespoons (60 g) butter* | Stir in the chicken broth, sage sprigs, and porcini tea and transfer everything to a 9" x 13" (23 cm x 33 cm) baking dish. Cover tightly with aluminum foil and cook for about 1½ hours, turning the meat every 30 minutes, until the turkey is tender. Keep the sauté pan for later. |
| *20 parsley sprigs, picked and chopped (about 6 tablespoons)* | |
| *12 thyme sprigs, picked and chopped (about 2 teaspoons)* | |
| *2 oz (57 g) Grana Padano, grated (about ¾ cup)* | When the pasta dough has rested, make the pappardelle (see p. 179). |

Bring a large pot of cold water to a boil.

When the turkey is cool enough to handle, pick the meat off the bone and return it to the braising liquid. Transfer the meat, liquid, and vegetables to the sauté pan and turn the heat to medium.

Drop the peas into boiling salted water. After 4 minutes, drop the pappardelle and cook, stirring frequently, until the pasta is almost al dente.

Drain the pappardelle 2 minutes before they are al dente, reserving 1 cup (237 ml) cooking water. The pasta will cook for the last few minutes in the sauce and absorb its flavors.

Transfer the pappardelle to the turkey sauce. Add the butter, parsley, and thyme and simmer the pasta in the sauce for about 2 minutes, adding cooking water as necessary and stirring frequently to avoid sticking. Serve immediately with freshly grated Grana.

# SPAGHETTI ALLA CHITARRA

On a well-floured surface, flatten the dough balls into a rectangular shape using a rolling pin until the dough is roughly ¼-inch (.5-cm) thick.

Open the rollers of the pasta machine to the widest setting. Run the dough through the machine 3 times, gradually adjusting the setting of the rollers to the next thinnest setting, until the dough is about half of its initial thickness. Make sure to keep the dough parallel with the edges of the rollers and use flour as necessary to prevent sticking.

Fold the ends of the dough into the center, making sure the width of the dough does not exceed the width of the rollers. Repeat the above process in its entirety 2 additional times until the dough is ⅛-inch (.3-cm) thick. It will be thicker than the pasta sheets used for making noodles (see page 169).

Cut the sheets into 12-inch (30-cm) lengths. You should get about eight 12-inch (30-cm)-long sheets per batch of dough. Put sheets on a floured surface or baking sheet and dust with flour in between each sheet so they don't stick together. Place a clean dishtowel on top of the sheets to prevent the dough from drying.

Place one sheet at a time on the chitarra and roll over the strings with a rolling pin. Twist the spaghetti alla chitarra into braids or nests and place them on a floured sheet tray or rimmed baking sheet. Place a clean dishtowel on top of the spaghetti to prevent the pasta from drying.

# SPAGHETTI ALLA CHITARRA ALLA PECORARA ABRUZZESE

## GUITAR STRING SPAGHETTI WITH RAGÙ ABRUZZESE

———

*This dish is a little time consuming, but the results are entirely worth it. The combination of the bold flavors of lamb and peppers is one of my favorites. This is a robust mountainous braised lamb and pepper ragù, delicious with either pecorino Romano or dotted with fresh sheep's milk ricotta. Spaghetti alla chitarra is a fresh egg pasta rolled out on a machine with guitar-like strings that cut the thick sheets of pasta into ⅛-inch (.3-cm) square noodles. In the unlikely event that you don't have a chitarra (!), roll out the dough ⅛-inch (.3-cm)-thick and cut it into ⅛-inch-thick spaghetti.*

*1 batch Egg Pasta (see p. 152)*

*¼ cup (60 ml) extra virgin olive oil*

*1 medium yellow onion, cut into 1-inch (2.5-cm) dice*

*2 celery stalks, cut into 1-inch (2.5-cm) dice*

*2 red or yellow bell peppers, cut into 1-inch (2.5-cm) dice*

*3 garlic cloves, smashed*

*1½ lbs (680 g) lamb shoulder, cut into 1-inch (2.5-cm) dice*

*2 rosemary sprigs, picked*

*1 cup (237 ml) dry white wine, like a Trebbiano or a Frascati*

*¼ cup (60 ml) saffron water (see p. 245)*

Preheat the oven to 275°F (130°C).

Put 2 tablespoons olive oil in a 14-inch (36-cm) sauté pan over medium-high heat. Add the onion, celery, peppers, garlic, and a pinch of salt and cook for at least 10 minutes, stirring occasionally, until the vegetables just start to soften. Remove the vegetables and set them aside on a plate.

Put 2 tablespoons olive oil in the same pan, keep it over medium-high heat, and add the lamb. Brown the meat all over for about 15 minutes, stirring occasionally, then add the rosemary, white wine, and saffron water and let the liquid reduce by half. Return the vegetables to the pan and add the tomato puree. Bring to a simmer and turn off the heat. Taste and adjust the seasoning.

Transfer the ingredients to a 9" x 13" (23 cm x 33 cm) baking dish and add about 1½ cups broth. Cover the baking dish tightly with aluminum foil or with a lid. Braise the meat for about 3 hours, stirring every hour,

*28 oz (794 g) canned whole San Marzano-style tomatoes, pureed with a hand blender or in a food processor*

*2 cups (473 ml) lamb or chicken broth (see pp. 234–35)*

*2 oz (57 g) pecorino Romano, grated (about ½ cup)*

until the lamb is very tender. Add more broth or water if the sauce level is more than halfway below the meat. Make sure the meat is at least halfway submerged in liquid at all times.

Prepare the Egg Pasta (see p. 153).

When the pasta dough has rested, make the Spaghetti alla Chitarra (see p. 199).

When the meat is tender and the Spaghetti alla Chitarra are ready, bring a large pot of cold water to a boil.

Put the sauce in a 14-inch (36-cm) high-sided sauté pan over medium-low heat.

Drop the Spaghetti alla Chitarra into boiling salted water and cook, stirring frequently, until the pasta is almost al dente. (The pasta will cook for the last few minutes in the sauce and absorb its flavors.) Drain the spaghetti 2 minutes before they are al dente, reserving 1 cup (237 ml) cooking water.

Transfer the Spaghetti alla Chitarra to the sauce. Turn the heat to medium-high and simmer the pasta in the sauce for about 2 minutes, adding cooking water as necessary and stirring frequently to avoid sticking. Serve immediately with freshly grated pecorino.

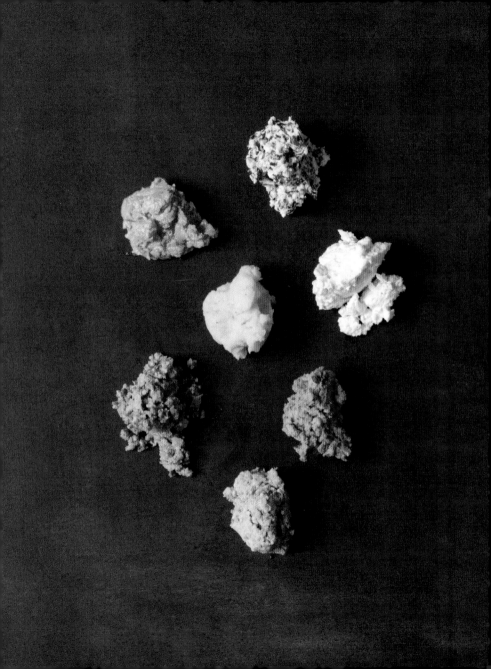

# PASTA RIPIENA

## FILLED PASTA

There are many types of filled pasta of varying sizes, shapes, and fillings. Each region or even town has its favorite. In Northern Italy, you'll likely find pasta filled with meat, while pasta stuffed with vegetables is more characteristic of Southern Italy.

The dough used to make filled pasta is wetter than that used to make unfilled pasta so that it won't dry out or become brittle while you are filling and sealing each piece. Make sure you work with only one sheet of pasta a time and keep the rest of the sheets covered with a dish towel until you're ready to use them so they remain moist. Work as quickly and efficiently as you can (you'll fall into a pasta making rhythm) so the pasta doesn't dry out or crack. The Green Pasta Dough is naturally wetter than the basic Egg Pasta Dough because the greens puree keeps it extra moist.

Keep the dough-to-filling ratio in mind (each recipe in this book gives an estimate of the amount of filling for that specific shape). You want each piece to be nicely stuffed without being overfilled, or else you risk tearing the dough as you shape it or you risk having the filled pasta explode while it cooks. Similarly, you don't want to under stuff the pasta, or the balance of flavors will be off and the amount of dough will feel excessive.

Once you've filled the pasta, carefully seal it at the edges and around the filling, gently pressing down with your fingers so that air pockets don't form and the filling doesn't fall out as the pasta cooks.

I always like to use a spoon and my hands to fill ravioli, especially for meat fillings, but a piping bag is great for ricotta or softer vegetable fillings.

Filled pasta should be used within 24 hours or can be frozen for up to two weeks.

# RAVIOLI

Sheet and laminate the dough (see p. 169).

Fold the sheet halfway along its length to form a crease.

Dot one half of the sheet with 1 tablespoon-sized portions of filling spread evenly every ½ inch (1.2 cm).

Brush the sheets in between the filling with water.

Fold the other half of the sheet over the filling. Do not seal the edges yet.

Starting at the bottom edge, use your thumb and forefinger to gently pinch out the air moving systematically from left to right, working in rows.

Using a fluted edged cutter, cut the ravioli into squares.

Place the ravioli on a floured, rimmed baking sheet. Place a clean dishtowel on top of the pasta to prevent it from drying.

# RAVIOLI DI RICOTTA CON CONSERVA DI POMODORO ESTIVO

## RICOTTA RAVIOLI WITH TOMATO CONFIT

*This dish might be the best fresh pasta dish on the planet. Seriously. The light fluffy sheep's milk ricotta seasoned simply with salt and pepper and a little bit of Grana contrasted with smashed tomato and an herb oil is a revelation.*

*A tomato* conserva, *from the verb* conservare, *is used in this recipe. You can make these tomatoes up to 4 days in advance. This recipe works best with Early Girl or cherry tomatoes; the high acidity helps to balance the poaching herb oil and fluffy ricotta. Don't use a San Marzano tomato, which is a pulpy fleshy tomato better suited for making sauce.*

*The leftover oil (and you'll have lots) may be used for a new batch of tomatoes or, in everyday cooking, to make any* soffritto. *The tomato oil adds a delicious subtle herb and tomato background in any dish.*

*1 batch Wet Egg Pasta (see p. 152) (to yield 10-12 ravioli per person)*

*6 Italian basil sprigs*

*6 summer savory or thyme sprigs*

*2 bay leaves*

*10 Early Girl tomatoes or 40 cherry tomatoes, concassé but kept whole (see p. 240)*

*4 cups (946 ml) extra virgin olive oil*

*2 lbs (907 g) fresh sheep's milk ricotta*

*1½ oz (43 g) Grana Padano, grated (about ½ cup)*

*Freshly ground black pepper, to taste*

*Freshly ground nutmeg, to taste*

Prepare the Wet Egg Pasta (see p. 153).

Preheat the oven to 250°F (120°C).

Prepare the tomato concassé: put the herbs in a small high-sided baking dish and place the tomatoes on top of the bed of herbs. The tomatoes should be tightly packed. Season them with salt and set aside for 20 minutes to allow the salt to be absorbed.

After 20 minutes cover the tomatoes with the olive oil and bake for 2½ to 3 hours or until the tomatoes are very soft and tender. Make sure the tomatoes are fully submerged in oil at all times or else they can dry out or burn. Add more oil if necessary.

Prepare the ricotta filling: in a medium bowl, combine the ricotta and Grana. Adjust the seasoning with salt, pepper, and nutmeg.

When the pasta dough has rested, prepare the ravioli (see p. 205).

When the tomatoes are meltingly tender, bring a large pot of cold water to a boil.

Drop the ravioli into boiling salted water and cook, stirring frequently, until the pasta is al dente. Drain the ravioli and transfer them to a bowl. Toss them with ¼ cup (60 ml) of the tomato conserva oil. Spoon the tomatoes over the ravioli, pressing down on the tomatoes slightly until they release their juices, and drizzle with a little more conserva oil if you like. Serve immediately.

# RAVIOLI DI PATATE, AGLIO FRESCO E ERBA CIPOLLINA

## GREEN GARLIC AND POTATO RAVIOLI WITH

### BUTTER & CHIVES

———

*Green garlic usually shows up around February. It's the first glimpse of green, signaling that spring is finally on its way. This is a Chez Panisse–inspired recipe that reinvents an Italian classic. The community at the American Academy loves it.*

*1 batch Wet Egg Pasta (see p. 152) (to yield 10-12 ravioli per person)*

*2 lbs (907 g) russet or Yukon gold potatoes, peeled and cut into 1-inch (2.5-cm) dice*

*½ cup (118 ml) extra virgin olive oil*

*1 bunch green garlic, green part removed and white part cut into ¼-inch (.6-cm) dice (about 2 cups)*

*3 oz (85 g) Grana Padano, grated (about 1 cup)*

*Freshly ground black pepper, to taste*

*8 tablespoons (120 g) butter*

*1 bunch chives, minced*

Prepare the Wet Egg Pasta (see p. 153).

Bring a large pot of cold water to a boil.

Prepare the filling for the ravioli: when the water comes to a rolling boil, salt it and blanch the potatoes until the edges are fuzzy, and the potatoes are tender. Drain them and lay the potatoes out on a baking sheet to cool slightly for 5 minutes.

Put the olive oil and green garlic and a pinch of salt in a 14-inch (36-cm) sauté pan over low heat. Cook, stirring occasionally, until the green garlic is translucent. Puree the cooked green garlic in a food processor or with a hand blender.

Pass the potatoes through a food mill or mash them with a fork. In a medium mixing bowl, combine the green garlic puree and the potatoes. Keep the sauté pan for later. Add half of the Grana. Taste and adjust the seasoning with salt and a generous amount of freshly ground black pepper.

When the pasta dough has rested, prepare the ravioli (see p. 205).

Bring a large pot of cold water to a boil.

Drop the ravioli into boiling salted water and cook, stirring frequently, until the pasta is almost al dente.

Put the butter, chives, and ½ cup (60 ml) cooking water in the sauté pan over low heat, swirling the pan until the butter has emulsified into the water, then turn the heat off.

Drain the ravioli 2 minutes before they are al dente, reserving ½ cup (118 ml) cooking water. The pasta will cook for the last few minutes in the sauce and absorb its flavors. Transfer the ravioli to the sauce. Turn the heat to low and simmer the ravioli in the sauce for about 2 minutes, tossing well to avoid sticking and adding cooking water as necessary, until the pasta is coated with the sauce. Serve immediately with the remaining freshly grated Grana.

# RAVIOLI DI RICOTTA E ORTICHE CON BURRO E SALVIA

## STINGING NETTLE AND SHEEP'S MILK RICOTTA RAVIOLI WITH BUTTER & SAGE

———

*This is one of our interpretations of ravioli in* magro, *meaning that they are lean, thus made without meat, but instead of using ricotta and spinach, as is traditional, we use nettles and a green pasta dough. Adding water to the butter allows the butter solids to emulsify and creates a velvety sauce. Use latex or rubber gloves when cleaning stinging nettles. Strip the leaves off the stems, discarding only the tough woody stems.*

*1 batch Green Pasta (see p. 152)
(to yield 10-12 ravioli per person)*

*4 tablespoons extra virgin olive oil*

*1 lb (454 g) nettles, picked*

*3 oz (85 g) Grana Padano, grated (about 1 cup)*

*1 lb (454 g) sheep's milk ricotta*

*Freshly ground black pepper, to taste*

*Freshly ground nutmeg, to taste*

*8 medium sage leaves*

*8 tablespoons (120 g) butter*

Prepare the Green Pasta (see p. 153).

Put 2 tablespoons olive oil, the nettles, and a pinch of salt in a 14-inch (36-cm) sauté pan over low heat. Cook, stirring occasionally, until the nettles have wilted and are tender. Transfer the nettles to a baking sheet to cool.

When the nettles are cool enough to handle, chop them.

Prepare the filling: in a large mixing bowl combine 2 tablespoons olive oil, ½ cup Grana, the chopped nettles, and the ricotta. Adjust the seasoning with more Grana, salt, pepper, and a touch of nutmeg.

When the pasta dough has rested, prepare the ravioli (see p. 205).

Bring a large pot of cold water to a boil.

Drop the ravioli into boiling salted water and cook, stirring frequently.

Meanwhile, put the butter, sage, and ½ cup (118 ml) cooking water in a 14-inch (36-cm) sauté pan over medium-low heat. Cook, swirling the pan, until the butter has emulsified into the water, then turn the heat off.

Drain the ravioli 2 minutes before they are al dente. (The pasta will cook for the last few minutes in the sauce and absorb its flavors.) Transfer the ravioli to the sauce, and turn the heat to medium. Simmer the pasta in the sauce for 1 or 2 minutes, tossing well until the pasta is coated with the butter sauce. Serve immediately with the remaining Grana.

# RAVIOLI DI CASTAGNE CON PORCINI
## CHESTNUT RAVIOLI WITH PORCINI MUSHROOMS

*Alfredo Gianfrocca is the caretaker of the Villa Aurelia and is an avid mushroom forager. One fall, when several pounds of porcini were delivered to the kitchen, Alfredo explained that the lighter brown porcini grow near oak and pine trees, while the darker porcini, the ones with deep brown caps, grow under chestnut trees. Alfredo also told me that the darker are the most sought after type of porcini because they are the most flavorful. I loved hearing this because at the RSFP we always teach "what grows together goes together," and so it's no coincidence that porcini and chestnuts seem made for each other.*

*1 batch Chestnut Pasta Dough
(see p. 152)
(to yield 10-12 ravioli per person)*

*8 oz (227 g) whole chestnuts*

*2 lbs (907 g) fresh sheep's milk
ricotta*

*1½ oz (43 g) Grana Padano,
grated (about ½ cup),
plus more for serving*

*Freshly ground black pepper,
to taste*

*Freshly ground nutmeg, to taste*

*¼ cup (60 ml) extra virgin
olive oil*

*2 tablespoons (30 g) butter*

*2 lbs (907 g) porcini mushrooms,
cleaned and sliced ¼-inch
thick (.6 cm) (see p. 245)*

*20 parsley sprigs, picked and
chopped (about 6 tablespoons)*

Bring a medium pot of cold water to a boil.

Score the chestnuts with an X on the flat part of the skin. When the water comes to a rolling boil, add the chestnuts and boil them for 5 to 10 minutes, or until the skins begin to split, and drain them.

When the chestnuts are cool, peel them using a paring knife, chop them, and set aside.

Prepare the chestnut pasta (see p. 153).

Make the ricotta filling: combine the ricotta and Grana. Taste and adjust the seasoning with salt, pepper, and nutmeg.

When the pasta dough has rested, prepare the ravioli (see p. 205).

Put the olive oil and butter in a 14-inch (36-cm) sauté pan over medium-high heat.

When the butter begins to foam, add the porcini. Sauté until the mushrooms start to brown slightly. Turn the heat to low, add the chestnuts and continue cooking for 3 more minutes, or until the mushrooms are completely tender. Add the parsley and season with salt and pepper only at the end so that the mushrooms maintain a firm texture. Turn off the heat and set the pan aside.

Drop the ravioli into boiling salted water and cook, stirring frequently, until the pasta is al dente. Drain the ravioli, reserving ¼ cup (60 ml) cooking water. Transfer them to the pan and toss well, adding cooking water as necessary. Serve immediately with freshly grated Grana.

# CAPPELLACCI

Sheet and laminate the dough (see p. 169).

Cut the sheets into 2½-inch (6-cm) squares.

Fill each square with 1 teaspoon of filling.

Brush the edges of the squares with water.

Fold the bottom left corner onto the top right corner to form a stuffed triangle. Gently pinch the air out and seal the edges.

Place your forefinger over the filling and wrap the cappellaccio around your finger bringing the bottom edges to the front and pinching them together.

Place the cappellacci on a floured rimmed baking sheet. Place a clean dishtowel on top of the pasta to prevent it from drying.

# CAPPELLACCI DI ZUCCA ALLA FERRARESE

## BUTTERNUT SQUASH CAPPELLACCI WITH
## BROWN BUTTER, BITTER ALMONDS & SAGE

———

*In Ferrara this kind of filled pasta is called cappellacci because it resembles a large pointy hat (cappello in Italian). There are many different ways to prepare butternut squash ravioli. Although cappellacci are traditionally filled with butternut squash and bitter almonds and are usually served with brown butter and sage, sometimes fruit mostarda is added to the butternut squash, or sometimes the cappellacci are served with a hearty ragù Bolognese.*

*1 batch Wet Egg Pasta (see p. 152) (to yield 10-12 cappellacci per person)*

*1½ lbs (680 kg) butternut squash*

*12 tablespoons (180 g) butter*

*16 sage leaves, 8 leaves thinly sliced (8 left whole)*

*2 bitter almond cookies, ground in a food processor, or ¾ teaspoon bitter almond extract*

*1 oz (28 g) Grana Padano, grated (about ⅓ cup), plus more for serving*

*Freshly ground black pepper, to taste*

*Freshly ground nutmeg, to taste*

Prepare the Wet Egg Pasta (see p. 153).

Preheat the oven to 350°F (175°C).

Cut the butternut squash in half and remove the seeds. Place each half cut side down on a baking sheet or in a roasting pan lined with parchment paper. Roast for at least 1 hour, or until the thickest part of the squash is completely soft to the touch.

When the squash is cool enough to handle, scoop out the flesh and put it in a bowl.

Make the brown butter: place a small saucepot over medium heat with 8 tablespoons of butter and allow it to melt, swirling the pan so the butter melts evenly, until the solids start to turn golden brown. It will have a pleasant nutty aroma. Turn off the heat to halt the cooking and skim the foam off the surface. Pay close attention since the butter can go from golden brown to burnt very quickly. If you burn the butter, discard it and start over. Immediately add the sliced sage leaves to the golden brown butter and let sizzle for 30 seconds. Add the butter, bitter almond cookies or extract, and 3 tablespoons of Grana to the squash, and stir until a smooth puree has formed. You may also use a food processor to obtain a smooth puree if necessary. Season the puree with salt, pepper, and a touch of nutmeg. Taste and adjust the seasoning.

When the pasta dough has rested, prepare the cappellacci (see p. 215).

Bring a large pot of cold water to a boil.

Put 4 tablespoons of butter in a 14-inch (36-cm) sauté pan over medium heat until you obtain brown butter (just like before). When the butter is golden brown, add ¼ cup (60 ml) cooking water along with the whole sage leaves and turn off the heat.

Drop the cappellacci into boiling salted water and cook, stirring frequently, until they are al dente. Drain the cappellacci and transfer them to the sauté pan. Toss until they are coated with the brown butter and serve immediately with the remaining Grana.

# TORTELLINI

Sheet and laminate the dough (see p. 169).

Cut the sheets into 1½-inch (4-cm) squares.

Fill each square with ¼ teaspoon of filling.

Brush the edges of the squares with water.

Fold the bottom left corner onto the top right corner to form a stuffed triangle. Gently pinch the air out and seal the edges.

Wrap the triangle, point side up, around the nail of your index finger. Join the two bottom edges of the triangle under your index finger and pinch them together to seal them with your thumb.

Place the tortellini on a floured rimmed baking sheet. Place a clean dishtowel on top of the pasta to prevent it from drying.

# TORTELLINI IN BRODO

## TORTELLINI SERVED IN BROTH

———

*Tortellini in Brodo hail from Bologna in Emilia-Romagna. As with Ragù alla Bolognese, this is such a serious dish that an official recipe was registered with the Chamber of Commerce in Bologna on December 7, 1974. Tortellini in Brodo seems to me to be the ultimate winter food. Pasta in Brodo is so soothing that Italians always serve it to loved ones when they are sick with a cold. Tortellini in Brodo are also associated with festive occasions; on Christmas Day they are traditionally served in capon broth.*

*There are multiple legends linked to the tortellino shape, and my favorite story goes something like this: the goddess Venus once came to stay at an inn near Bologna. The innkeeper fell madly in love with her and peeked into her room while she was sleeping. He was so entranced by the beauty of her body that the next morning he created these tortellini that were in the shape of Venus' perfect navel. In Bologna tortellini are often called Ombelichi di Venere, Venus' Navels.*

*This is the RSFP's take on the classic Bolognese dish. We've come to think of the proportions in this recipe as a "golden ratio" of cured meats and Parmigiano-Reggiano. Make sure you use a food processor to grind your cured meats as finely as possible.*

---

*1 batch Wet Egg Pasta (see p. 152) (to yield 15-20 tortellini per person)*

*6 oz (170 g) Prosciutto di Parma, finely ground*

*6 oz (170 g) mortadella, finely ground*

*6 oz (170 g) prosciutto cotto or ham, finely ground*

*4 oz (113 g) Parmigiano-Reggiano, grated (about 1½ cups), plus more for serving*

*Freshly ground black pepper, to taste*

Prepare the Wet Egg Pasta (see p. 153).

Make the tortellini filling: in a large mixing bowl, combine the prosciutto di Parma, mortadella, prosciutto cotto, and Parmigiano. Taste and adjust the seasoning with salt, pepper, and a touch of nutmeg.

When the pasta dough has rested, make the tortellini (see p. 219).

Bring a large pot of cold water to a boil, and bring a medium pot of broth to a boil.

Drop the tortellini into boiling salted water and cook, stirring frequently, for 2 minutes. Drain the tortellini and transfer them to the pot of broth. Turn the heat to medium so the tortellini simmer in the liquid until they are

*Ground nutmeg, to taste*

*6 cups (1.4 l) beef broth
(to make your own see p. 235)*

*10 parsley sprigs, picked and
chopped (about 3 tablespoons)*

al dente. Garnish with parsley and serve
immediately with lots of broth and more
freshly grated Parmigiano.

# AGNOLOTTI

Sheet and laminate the dough (see p. 169).

Fold the sheet halfway along its width to form a crease.

Dot one half of the sheet with 1 teaspoon-sized portions of filling spread evenly every ½-inch (1.2-cm) on the crease line.

Brush the sheets in between the filling with water.

Fold the other half of the sheet over the filling. Do not seal the edges yet.

Starting at the bottom edge, use your thumb and forefinger to gently pinch out the air moving systematically from left to right.

Using a fluted-edge cutter, cut the agnolotti into squares with the filling right at the crease.

Place the agnolotti on a floured rimmed baking sheet. Place a clean dishtowel on top of the pasta to prevent it from drying.

# AGNOLOTTI CON BURRO E SALVIA
## AGNOLOTTI WITH BUTTER AND SAGE

---

*In the United States, cow meat is sold as either veal or beef, but Italians love something in between called* vitellone, *which literally means large veal. In Italy veal is butchered before it is 12 months old, vitellone between 12 and 18 months of age, and beef when the cow is 3 or 4 years old. Vitellone meat is darker and more flavorful than veal, yet it is more tender and delicate than beef.*

*Agnolotti come from Piedmont in northern Italy. You'll find them in various shapes and sizes, but the filling is traditionally placed at the bottom edge of the pasta dough, instead of in the middle (like ravioli). There are many different versions of agnolotti, but they are typically filled with some combination of chopped-up leftover roasted or braised meat, cabbage or endive, egg, and Grana. Some versions include rice or white truffles. Agnolotti are classically served in broth, with butter and sage and even white truffles, or with the sauce left over from the roast or braised meat.*

*We're giving you a recipe from scratch here, but you can definitely make these with leftover roast meat.*

1 batch Wet Egg Pasta (see p. 152)
(to yield 10-12 agnolotti
per person)

2 tablespoons extra virgin
olive oil

1 small yellow onion, minced

12 thyme sprigs, picked and
chopped (about 2 teaspoons)

9 oz (255 g) veal or vitellone,
ground

5 oz (142 g) pork shoulder or
pancetta, ground

¼ cup (59 ml) dry white wine,
preferably a Roero Arneis
from the Langhe

Prepare the Wet Egg Pasta (see p. 153).

Bring a medium pot of cold water to a boil.

Make the agnolotti filling: put 1 tablespoon olive oil, the onion, and a pinch of salt in a 14-inch (36-cm) sauté pan over medium-low heat. After 2 minutes, add the thyme and cook, stirring occasionally, until the onion is translucent. Transfer the onions to a plate. Add 1 tablespoon olive oil, the veal and pork to the sauté pan and turn the heat to medium-high. Cook, stirring frequently and breaking up the meat with a wooden spoon, until it has wept its juices. Add the white wine and cook until the liquid has evaporated. Remove the meat from the pan and put it on a baking sheet to cool.

14 oz (397 g) green cabbage, leaves kept whole

1 egg yolk

Freshly ground black pepper, to taste

Freshly ground nutmeg, to taste

2 teaspoons grated Grana Padano, plus more for serving

4 tablespoons (60 g) butter

8 sage leaves

When the water comes to a rolling boil, salt it and blanch the cabbage leaves until tender. Drain it and spread the cabbage out on a baking sheet to cool. When the cabbage is cool enough to handle, squeeze out any excess water and finely dice it.

In a medium mixing bowl, combine the onions, meat, cabbage, egg yolk, and Grana. Taste and adjust the seasoning with salt, pepper, and a touch of nutmeg.

When the pasta dough has rested, prepare the agnolotti (see p. 223).

Bring a large pot of cold water to a boil.

Put the butter and ¼ cup (60 ml) cooking water in a 14-inch (36-cm) sauté pan over low heat, swirling the pan until the butter has emulsified into the water, then turn the heat off. Add the sage leaves.

Drop the agnolotti into boiling salted water and cook, stirring occasionally. Drain the agnolotti 2 minutes before they are al dente, reserving ¼ cup (60 ml) cooking water.

Transfer the pasta to the sauté pan and turn the heat to medium. Toss the ravioli with the butter and sage, adding cooking water as necessary, until the agnolotti are coated with the sauce. Serve immediately with freshly grated Grana.

# LASAGNE AL POMODORO FRESCO
## SUMMER LASAGNE WITH TOMATOES,
## MOZZARELLA & BASIL

———

*This is a great summer dish and a twist on the classic versions. Lasagne often takes hours of preparation, yet this take on lasagne is surprisingly quick and easy to make. The neat trick is that juicy summer tomatoes and fresh mozzarella provide the liquid in which the pasta sheets cook. There's no need to blanch the pasta sheets in advance. Make sure you let the lasagne rest before serving so it has time to set.*

1 batch Egg Pasta (see p. 152)

2 lbs (907 g) fresh mozzarella, cut into ¼-inch (.6-cm) cubes

4 oz (113 g) Grana Padano, grated (about 1¼ cups)

4 lbs (1.8 kg) San Marzano or Roma tomatoes, quartered, or cherry tomatoes, cut in half

20 Italian basil leaves

¼ cup (60 ml) extra virgin olive oil, plus 1 tablespoon

1 teaspoon hot pepper flakes

Prepare the Egg Pasta (see p. 153).

When the pasta dough has rested, roll it out into sheets (see p. 169).

Combine the mozzarella and Grana in a bowl. The Grana helps to absorb the moisture of the mozzarella and creates an even browning crust of cheese as it bakes.

Puree the tomatoes and the basil in a blender or in a bowl using a hand blender. Taste and adjust the seasoning with salt and hot pepper flakes. Stir in ¼ cup olive oil.

Preheat the oven to 375°F (190°C).

Assemble the lasagne: drizzle the bottom of a 9" x 13" (23 cm x 33 cm) Pyrex dish with 1 tablespoon olive oil. Put a thin layer of tomato puree on the bottom of the dish. Make sure you dust off all the flour from the sheets before using them. Alternate layers of pasta sheets, tomato puree, and cheese. Repeat the process 5 times to obtain 6 layers total.

Bake the lasagne for about 45 minutes, or until a thick golden crust has formed. Cool for at least 1 hour before serving.

# CANNELLONI DI RICOTTA E SPINACI
## CANNELLONI WITH SHEEP'S MILK RICOTTA & SPINACH

*We make these cannelloni with any greens we have handy. Chard, nettles, turnip tops, cavolo nero, and kale all work well. We prefer to use wild greens. There is no need for besciamella (béchamel) since the ricotta and spinach provide a creamy and airy filling.*

*1 batch Egg Pasta (see p. 152)*

*5 tablespoons extra virgin olive oil*

*3 garlic cloves, smashed*

*1 lb (454 g) spinach*

*1 lb (454 g) sheep's milk ricotta*

*3 oz (85 g) Grana Padano, grated (about 1 cup)*

*Freshly ground black pepper, to taste*

*Ground nutmeg, to taste*

*28 oz (794 g) canned whole San Marzano-style tomatoes, pureed with a hand blender or in a food processor*

*1 lb (454 g) fresh mozzarella, cut into ¼-inch (.6-cm) cubes*

Prepare the Egg Pasta (see p. 153).

Put 2 tablespoons olive oil and the garlic in a 14-inch (36-cm) sauté pan over medium-low heat. Cook, stirring occasionally, until the garlic is just golden, then remove and discard it.

Add the spinach and cook, stirring frequently, until it is just wilted. Remove the spinach and lay it out on a baking sheet to dissipate the heat.

When the pasta dough has rested, roll it out into sheets (see p. 169).

Bring a large pot of cold water to a boil.

When the water comes to rolling boil, prepare a large bowl of cold water. Blanch the sheets in batches in salted boiling water for 2 minutes. Remove the sheets from the water using a slotted spoon and transfer them immediately to the large bowl of cold water to stop the cooking process.

When the spinach is cool enough to handle, squeeze out any excess water and chop it.

In a medium mixing bowl, combine 2 tablespoons olive oil, the ricotta, ¾ cup Grana, and the chopped spinach. Taste and adjust the seasoning with salt, pepper, and nutmeg.

Lay the sheets out on a clean surface or cutting board and pat them dry with a dishtowel. Cut each 12-inch (30 cm) sheet of pasta into 3" x 4" (8 cm x 10 cm) rectangles.

Fill each rectangle with the spinach and ricotta filling and tightly roll the rectangle lengthwise. It should resemble a small rolled cigar.

Preheat the oven to 375°F (190°C).

Drizzle the bottom of a 9" x 13" inch (23 cm x 33 cm) baking dish with 1 tablespoon olive oil. Put a thin layer of tomato puree on the bottom of the dish. Place the cannelloni on top in rows. Pour the remaining tomato puree over the cannelloni so that they are completely covered. Dot with mozzarella and bake for 45 minutes, or until the mozzarella has formed a golden crust. Remove the cannelloni from the oven and sprinkle with ¼ cup Grana. Cool for 15 minutes before serving.

# CANNELLONI DI CARNE
## MEAT CANNELLONI WITH TOMATO SAUCE & MOZZARELLA

*I often find cannelloni to be heavy, but they don't need to be. The trick I like to use is to merely add a small amount of dense besciamella (béchamel) to the meat to bind the mixture, instead of layering the dish with besciamella for a creamy sauce, which is more traditional. The acid from the pureed tomatoes cuts through the meat and besciamella filling and makes this a light yet substantial dish.*

1 batch Egg Pasta (see p. 152)

2 tablespoons (30g) butter

1 oz (28 g) all-purpose flour

10 oz (295 ml) whole milk

Ground nutmeg, to taste

4 garlic cloves, smashed

5 tablespoons extra virgin olive oil

14 oz (397 g) beef chuck, ground

10 oz (283 g) pork shoulder, ground

6 oz (170 g) Grana Padano, grated (about 2 cups)

20 parsley sprigs, picked and chopped (about 6 tablespoons)

10 thyme or savory sprigs, picked and chopped (about 2 teaspoons)

28 oz (794 g) canned whole San Marzano-style tomatoes, pureed with a hand blender or in a food processor

Prepare the Egg Pasta (see p. 153).

Prepare the besciamella: melt the butter in a small saucepot over low heat. Add the flour and cook for 2 minutes, whisking constantly. Gradually add the milk and keep whisking to avoid forming lumps. Turn the heat to the lowest it can go and keep cooking and whisking consistently for about 20 minutes, until the besciamella is very thick. Taste and adjust the seasoning with salt and nutmeg. Set aside to cool.

Put 2 tablespoons of olive oil and the garlic in a 14-inch (36-cm) high-sided sauté pan over high heat. When the oil is hot, add half of the ground meat and cook, stirring occasionally, for about 10 minutes, or until the meat has browned. Remove the meat from the pan and set it aside.

Repeat the process with the remaining olive oil, garlic, and ground meat.

Season all the ground meat with salt and pepper, then remove and discard the garlic.

Combine the ground meat, besciamella, ½ cup Grana, and herbs in a large bowl. Taste and adjust the seasoning.

*1 lb (454 g) fresh mozzarella,
cut into ¼-inch (.6-cm) cubes*

*2 oz (57 g) Grana Padano, grated
(about ¾ cup)*

When the pasta dough has rested, roll it out into sheets (see p. 169).

Bring a large pot of cold water to a boil.

When the water comes to a rolling boil, prepare a large bowl of cold water. Blanch the pasta sheets in batches in salted boiling water for 2 minutes. Remove them from the water using a slotted spoon and transfer the sheets immediately to the large bowl of cold water to stop the cooking process.

Lay the sheets out on a clean surface or cutting board and pat them dry with a dishtowel. Cut each 12-inch (30.5-cm) sheet of pasta into 3" x 4" (8 cm x 10 cm) rectangles.

Fill each rectangle with the meat filling and tightly roll it lengthwise. It should resemble a small rolled cigar.

Preheat the oven to 375°F (190°C).

Drizzle the bottom of a 9" x 13" (23 cm x 33 cm) baking dish with 1 tablespoon olive oil. Put a thin layer of tomato puree on the bottom of the dish. Place the cannelloni on top in rows. Pour the remaining tomato puree over the cannelloni so that they are completely covered. Dot with mozzarella and bake for 45 minutes, or until the mozzarella has formed a golden crust.

Remove the cannelloni from the oven and sprinkle with ¼ cup (32 g) Grana. Cool for 15 minutes before serving.

# BASIC RECIPES
# & TECHNIQUES

# BRODO DI POLLO

## CHICKEN BROTH

---

*A full-flavored, balanced broth requires a combination of bones. Necks, wings, feet, and backs are especially good due to their gelatin content, which adds tremendous flavor and body. A "blond" broth (usually chicken) in which the meaty bones are thrown in raw lends a delicate, clean, and neutral flavor.*

*Use a high-sided large 10-quart (9.4-liter) stockpot and make sure the bones are constantly fully submerged in cold water. A broth must always be started using cold water, since the proteins in the bones gently coagulate as the water heats up and squeeze out their impurities, resulting in a clearer, cleaner broth. The first skimming should be done when only the bones have been added and the broth has nearly reached a simmer. You'll notice a thick dense grayish foam on the surface. These are the impurities that must be removed or they will sink back into the broth, making it cloudy with a muddy taste. Add the aromatics after the first skimming. Do not stir the broth as it cooks; this could also cloud it. Foam may reappear; keep skimming as the broth cooks consistently at a gentle simmer. (Any more heat can cause an emulsification, and any less results in an inferior extraction.) Set the pot slightly off center of the burner to create a natural convection current that allows the water to circulate, ensuring even cooking and better clarity, flavor, and extraction.*

4½ pounds (2 kg) chicken bones (backs, necks, wings, and feet)

Put the bones and cold water in a stockpot over medium heat.

6 quarts (5.7 l) cold water

When the water is hot but hasn't yet simmered, skim and discard the scum.

1 large carrot, peeled

2 celery stalks

Add the remaining ingredients and turn the heat to low so the broth cooks at a slow and gentle simmer. Cook for 3 hours without stirring. Skim the impurities as necessary.

1 large yellow onion, quartered

6 peppercorns

1 bay leaf

Strain the broth discarding the bones and let sit for 20 minutes. Skim the fat from the surface and use immediately, or let it cool completely and discard the congealed chicken fat on the surface. Refrigerate for up to 4 days, or freeze it and use within 3 weeks.

4 thyme sprigs

1 sage sprig

10 parsley stems, leaves removed and discarded

Pinch of salt

# BRODO DI MANZO O AGNELLO
## BEEF OR LAMB BROTH

———

*At the RSFP we encourage interns to taste the broth at three or four intervals as it cooks to track the development of flavor. They can taste the flavors improving steadily until the broth reaches its peak and has a perfect balance of flavor and brightness. After that, although it can continue to cook, at some point, it stops tasting better. It may taste stronger, but not better or brighter.*

*While a "blond" broth is rather delicate and light, roasting bones to make broth (usually for beef or lamb broth) adds a richer, deeper, and more developed flavor. Once you've roasted the bones, the procedure is the same as with chicken broth (see the headnote on the opposite page for a full description on how to prepare broth properly).*

4 pounds bones (1.8 kg) (ideally a combination of shanks, knuckles, tail, and/or lean chuck for beef, and a combination of shanks and neck for lamb)

6 quarts (5.7 l) cold water

1 large carrot, peeled

2 celery stalks

1 large yellow onion, quartered

1 tomato, quartered

6 peppercorns

1 bay leaf

4 thyme sprigs

10 parsley stems, leaves removed and discarded

Pinch of salt

Preheat the oven to 400F (200C). Roast the bones on a rimmed baking sheet for 1 hour and 15 minutes, or until the bones are a deep brown color.

Put the bones and cold water in a stockpot over medium heat. (Don't clean the baking sheet yet.)

Add 1 cup hot water to the baking sheet and scrape until the fondo has melted into the liquid and turned it golden brown. Add this liquid to the stockpot.

When the water is hot but hasn't yet simmered, skim and discard the scum.

Add the remaining ingredients and turn the heat to low so the broth cooks at a slow and gentle simmer. Cook for 3½ to 4 hours without stirring. Skim the impurities as necessary.

Strain the broth discarding the bones and let sit for 20 minutes. Skim the fat from the surface and use immediately, or let it cool completely and discard the congealed fat on the surface. Refrigerate for up to 4 days, or freeze it and use within 3 weeks.

# MOLLICA DI PANE

## BREADCRUMBS

_Homemade breadcrumbs are extremely versatile. I love them because of the crunch and texture they add to any dish. To my mind, breadcrumbs take dishes to the next level. They are delicious with beans, many types of pasta, salsa verde, and vegetables. This recipe makes about four cups of breadcrumbs. They keep well in an airtight container at room temperature for up to a week._

_1 pound 4 ounces day-old country bread (567 g), crust removed_

_⅓ cup (70 ml) olive oil_

Preheat the oven to 300°F (150°C).

Use a food processor to chop the bread into pebble-sized breadcrumbs.

Toss the breadcrumbs with the olive oil and sprinkle with salt to taste.

Spread the breadcrumbs into an even layer on a rimmed baking sheet and bake, stirring and checking every 5 minutes, until the breadcrumbs are perfectly golden brown, about 25 to 35 minutes.

# SALSICCIA

## SAUSAGE

_Contrary to popular belief, sausage is incredibly easy to make. It is essentially seasoned ground meat put into a casing. At the RSFP we make and case our own sausage, although when we use it for pasta, there is no need to put it into a casing because we break it up directly into the pan. Making sausage at home is a fun, simple, and easy process that will impress your guests. Store-bought sausage often has a variety of flavors and preservatives that could interfere with the simplicity of these recipes._

_The shoulder is often the preferred cut of meat to use for sausages because its meat-to-fat ratio is ideal. I recommend making the sausage in advance since the flavor of the seasoning becomes more pronounced with time._

_10 ounces (283 g) ground meat, like pork shoulder or lamb shoulder_

_1 teaspoon salt_

_½ teaspoon ground fennel seeds_

_¼ teaspoon freshly ground black pepper_

_½ teaspoon hot pepper flakes_

Combine the ground meat with the salt, fennel seeds, pepper, and hot pepper. Mix well with your hands for about 2 minutes, kneading as if you were making fresh pasta, to help distribute the seasoning evenly. Let the sausage rest in the refrigerator for at least 30 minutes before using it.

# PUREA VERDE

## GREENS PUREE

───

*Greens Puree is used when making green pasta dough; along with the egg, the greens puree serves as the liquid that binds with the flour. It gives the dough a wonderful deep-green color and a distinct flavor. I like to use Tuscan kale because of its intense color and taste that remain vibrant when it is cooked. I also love to use nettles. If you choose to make the puree with nettles, you'll probably need a little more than one-half pound. Make sure you use gloves to strip the leaves off the stems. The flavor of spinach and chard are also good, but they don't lend the same intense green color to the dough. There's no need to add salt to the puree, since it will be added to the pasta dough, but if you use the greens puree for anything else, season it to your liking.*

*We often serve pasta tossed with this greens puree for vegetarian dinners at the Academy. We like to add lots of olive oil, and top it with pecorino or ricotta salata. It's a great simple vegetarian dish.*

*½ lb (227 g) Tuscan or Lacinato kale, leaves stripped from the stems*

Bring a medium pot of cold water to a boil.

When the water comes to a rolling boil, add the kale leaves and cook until they are very tender. Drain them, reserving ½ cup cooking water. Spread the kale out on a baking sheet to dissipate the heat.

When the kale is cool enough to handle, squeeze out any excess water (it's ok if it remains a little wet) and chop it.

Puree it with a hand blender or in a food processor with about ¼ cup of the reserved cooking water, adding more as necessary, until you obtain a smooth puree. Pass the puree through a sieve to get rid of any fibrous strands that would remain visible in the pasta dough.

# SALSA DI POMODORO
## FRESH TOMATO SAUCE

———

Core and chop fresh tomatoes and put them in a large pot. Add a pinch of salt and stew them over medium heat until they have completely broken down, stirring frequently so they don't stick to the bottom of the pan. Then, pass the sauce through a food mill to remove the tough and bitter skins.

An alternate method is first to make tomato concassé, following the directions below, then add a pinch of salt, and stew down the tomatoes until they've turned into a sauce.

# POLPA DI POMODORO
## TOMATO CONCASSÉ

———

Bring a medium pot of cold water to a boil.

If you are using Early Girl tomatoes, score the bottoms of the tomatoes with an x and core them (this will help remove the skins once they are blanched). There is no need to go through this process for cherry tomatoes.

Lower a few tomatoes at a time into the boiling water. Let the tomatoes cook just long enough for the skins to loosen or blister slightly, about 15 seconds or less. Remove them quickly and transfer them to a bowl of ice-cold water. Repeat this process as needed. Once you have blanched all the tomatoes, remove them from the cold water and peel off the skins with your fingers or with a pairing knife. Finally, dice the tomatoes.

For the tomato concassé called for in Ravioli di Ricotta con Conserva di Pomodoro Estivo, make sure you keep the Early Girl or cherry tomatoes whole.

# PASSATA DI POMODORO
## TOMATO PUREE

———

To make tomato sauce, we always use canned whole San Marzano tomatoes that we puree ourselves. It is important that they are whole: canned diced or—even worse—canned pureed tomatoes tend to be watery and have less flavor than their canned whole counterparts. Avoid canned tomatoes with any added ingredients or flavors, such as "marinara sauce." You may find some with basil leaves, and that's fine. Make sure you use San Marzano, San Marzano-style, or plum canned tomatoes for the best, most intense taste.

Either carefully puree the tomatoes directly in the can using a hand blender, dump the contents of the whole can in a standing blender, or, if you prefer a chunkier sauce, fish out the tomatoes, chop them up, and add them back to the tomato liquid. For the most flavorful sauce, make sure you puree the tomatoes right before you use them.

# PESTO

*Pesto comes from the Italian word* pestare, *to pound. Many variations of pesto exist that combine different nuts, herbs, and cheeses, yet the technique remains the same. Traditionally, pesto is pounded in a marble mortar with a wooden pestle. Marble is classically used because it is an insulator and therefore remains cool. The wood pestle prevents both friction and the ingredients from heating up, which would cause them to oxidize. The ingredients are pounded separately; first the garlic, then the nuts, and finally the herbs. They are then mixed with olive oil and cheese. If you don't have a mortar and pestle, use a hand blender but do not use a food processor because it will not chop the leaves finely enough.*

*You can make pesto in advance and keep it in the refrigerator until you need it. It actually benefits from sitting a little—the flavors develop over time. Pesto will taste very different as soon as it is made, and after one hour, so always adjust the seasoning at the very last minute. I tend to use a very small amount of garlic since the essential oils of garlic bond with the fat molecules in olive oil (since fat bonds with fat) and the garlic flavor becomes more pronounced with time.*

For all pesto recipes in the book:
Put the garlic and a pinch of salt in the mortar and pound it until it turns into a paste. Remove and set it aside with a little olive oil to prevent oxidation.

Put the nuts in the mortar and pound them. Alternate between pounding and smearing in a circular motion until you obtain a chunky peanut butter—like consistency. Pound them more if you prefer a smoother pesto, but I like to keep it a little chunky. Remove the nuts and set them aside.

Carefully chop the herbs first (don't tear them) to avoid bruising them and put them in the mortar. Work in batches if the amount seems excessive. Pound the herbs until they have released some green liquid, then keep smearing in a circular motion, applying lots of pressure, until you get a smooth paste.

Stir in the nuts, garlic, cheese, and olive oil. Let the pesto sit for an hour in the refrigerator, then adjust the seasoning with olive oil, cheese, or salt as needed.

# PREPPING THE INGREDIENTS

## PEELING & SMASHING GARLIC

Many recipes in the book call for smashed garlic to infuse the *soffrito* and impart a more subtle garlic flavor than chopped garlic. Always prepare garlic right before you need it. If you prepare it in advance, make sure you cover it with a small amount of olive oil to preserve its flavors and ensure that it does not oxidize. The same goes for chopped garlic: always cover it with olive oil.

Remove the cloves from the garlic head. Cut the bottom off the clove and smash it, with the skin on, using either the heel of your palm or the thick part of your chef's knife. Smashing the clove first helps remove the skins easily. Remove the skin and the germ (usually a green sprout, although it can be white) inside the clove at its center. It's important to remove the germ, because it has a different consistency from the rest of the garlic; it can burn easily and make the oil taste bitter.

## RINSING CAPERS

Buy salt-packed capers: they have a more intense flavor than brined capers (capers sold in liquid), and the brine itself may interfere with the taste of your end product.

Rinse the capers in a fine-meshed strainer or skimmer under cold water until the salt has fallen off. Put the capers in a small pot, cover them with cold water, and put them over low heat. When the water comes to a simmer, turn off the heat and let the capers soak in the hot water for 15 to 20 minutes, then rinse them. Strain them and gently squeeze out any excess salty water. If the capers still seem too salty, repeat this process once or even twice.

## PLUMPING CURRANTS & RAISINS

Put the raisins and white wine in a small pot over low heat. Turn off the heat as soon as the wine comes to a boil. Let the raisins plump for at least 30 minutes in the hot wine. They are ready when they have absorbed all, or nearly all, of the wine.

## CLEANING ANCHOVIES

Buy salt-packed whole anchovies: they have a far more pure and distinct fish flavor than oil-packed fillets. If you buy a large can, take out as many anchovies as you will need for each recipe, and make sure the remaining anchovies are covered with salt. They keep well in the refrigerator for several months.

Rinse the anchovies under cold water, rubbing them delicately and shaking them in the water to remove the salt and the scales. Rinse and drain them at least five times, until the water is no longer murky, then let the anchovies soak in cool water for 15 to 20 minutes, depending on the size of the fish. This process plumps the anchovy and allows you to easily peel the fillets off the bone. Be careful not to over-plump the anchovies or they will taste water-logged. Clean the anchovies in a sink with trickling water. Slip a fingertip into the belly of the anchovy and rinse the cavity, removing the fish guts. Carefully pull one fillet off the spine and rinse it, then gently remove the dorsal and ventral fins. Drape the fillet over the side of a clean bowl to drip dry. Once you've peeled off the first fillet, carefully pull the spine off the second filet. Remove the dorsal and ventral fins once again. Rinse the fillet gently and drape it over the side of the bowl. Use immediately or cover with olive oil until needed. They will keep well in the refrigerator, under oil, for up to 3 days.

## CLEANING MUSHROOMS
Always store mushrooms in the refrigerator or somewhere cool. Keep them uncrowded in brown paper bags so they can breathe; never use plastic bags for mushrooms.

Don't worry too much about the mushrooms being a little dirty. If they are dry or close to dry, you won't have a problem cleaning them. Except for rare occasions, do no wash mushrooms—they easily become waterlogged and, once sautéed, will have a soggy boiled taste.

Pick off any pieces of dirt, or brush the mushrooms off with a dry tea-towel or with a brush (which is particularly great for cleaning gills), and use a paring knife to cut out chunks of dry dirt. Trim away any parts that looked bruised, discolored, or very soft.

If you're cleaning porcini, make sure to check under the cap to ensure that the sponge is firm and creamy-beige. If instead it looks greenish-brown, cut off this layer. Cut porcini open to check for worms (or wormholes) inside the mushroom, and cut off any affected areas.

## SAFFRON WATER
Put 1 teaspoon saffron threads and ¼ cup (60 ml) water or white wine in a small saucepan over very low heat. Bring to a boil and remove it immediately from the heat source. Infuse for 4 or 5 minutes before using.

## CLEANING ARTICHOKES
Prepare a large bowl with 1 gallon (3.8 liters) of water and squeeze the juice of 1 lemon directly in the bowl (add the lemon halves as well). The acidity of the

lemon juice prevents the artichokes from oxidizing and turning dark brown. Handle artichokes as quickly as possible, as they oxidize and turn brown as soon as they are peeled. Snap off the tough outer petals one at a time until you reach the pale colored petals of the heart of the artichoke. Cut off the top of the artichoke flower to about 1-inch (2.54 cm) above the base. Dip the artichoke in the lemon water and return it to your cutting board. Using a small knife, pare away the dark green layer (there is a paler green layer underneath) from the stem and around the base of the artichoke. Immediately dip the artichoke in the lemon water once again and return it to your cutting board. Cut the artichoke in half and scoop out the choke (fuzzy part of the heart) using a small spoon. Dip it in the lemon water once again and return it to your board. Slice the artichokes and drop them in the acidulated water until you need them. They will keep for up to 24 hours submerged in lemon water.

## COOKING TERMS

### BRAISING
To cook slowly in a small amount of liquid over low heat in a covered pot or pan on the stove or in the oven (usually the vegetables and/or meat are halfway submerged in liquid).

### SAUTÉING
To cook food quickly in a shallow pan with a small amount of fat over high heat. It is a technique in which the food is tossed or stirred frequently and kept moving almost constantly in the pan as it cooks; in French, the verb *sauter* means "to jump."

### SEARING OR BROWNING
To cook the surface of vegetables or meat over medium or high heat, turning them only occasionally, until brown.

### SIMMERING
Many recipes in this book call for simmering a sauce or simmering the pasta in the sauce for the last few minutes of cooking. A simmer is very different from a boil: boiling implies a fast, aggressive surface movement and constant burbling of liquid over high heat, while simmering means that there should be surface movement in the sauce or water in the form of sporadic bubbles that are just breaking on the surface over medium or low heat.

## SIZZLING

Sizzling is akin to frying, but at a much lower temperature. Sizzling is rather delicate, and takes a minute at most. It uses a higher intensity of heat than sweating, but lower than sautéing. We often refer to sizzling when we talk about adding herbs, garlic, capers, or anchovies to a soffritto. Sizzling is about rapidly infusing the oil with these additional flavors without burning or overcooking them. The oil sputters as you add the ingredients and makes a distinct soft sizzling sound. Listen carefully; as soon as the sound changes and becomes softer, immediately proceed with the recipe or the ingredients might burn.

## SWEATING

Sweating implies adding salt to vegetables from the beginning of the cooking process and cooking over relatively low heat. Salt serves to extract moisture. As the salted vegetable weeps its juices (much like sweat) and produces steam, the combination of salt and steam helps break the vegetables down slowly and cook them without adding color. Cover the pan with parchment paper or with a lid to sweat the vegetables over medium-low heat. Make sure there is a thick layer of vegetables when sweating them—a thin layer will cook too quickly and the vegetables could brown.

# BIBLIOGRAPHY

Bertolli, Paul, Gail Skoff, and Judy Dater. *Cooking by Hand*. New York: Clarkson Potter, 2003.

Bertolli, Paul. *Chez Panisse Cooking*. New York: Random House, 1988.

Bugialli, Giuliano. *Bugialli on Pasta*. New York: Simon and Schuster, 1988.

Cesari, Monica Saroni. *Italy Dish by Dish*. Trans. Susan Simon. New York: The Little Bookroom, 2011.

Downie, David. *Cooking the Roman Way: Authentic Recipes from the Home Cooks and Trattorias of Rome*. New York: Harper Collins, 2002.

Field, Carol. *The Italian Baker*. New York: Harper & Row, 1985.

Gho, Paola. *The Slow Food Dictionary to Italian Regional Cooking*. Bra, Italy: Slow Food Editor, 2010.

Hazan, Marcella. *Essentials of Classic Italian Cooking*. New York: A.A. Knopf, 1992.

Hildebrand, Caz, and Jacob Kenedy. *The Geometry of Pasta*. Philadelphia: Quirk, 2010.

Kasper, Lynne Rossetto. *The Splendid Table: Recipes from Emilia-Romagna, the Heartland of Northern Italian Food*. New York: W. Morrow, 1992.

Keller, Thomas, Dave Cruz, Susie Heller, Michael Ruhlman, and Amy Vogler. *Ad Hoc at Home*. New York: Artisan, 2009.

Locatelli, Giorgio, and Sheila Keating. *Made in Italy: Food & Stories*. New York: Ecco, 2007.

McGee, Harold. *Food and Cooking: An Encyclopedia of Kitchen Science, History and Culture*. London: Hodder and Stoughton, 2004.

Plotkin, Fred. *The Authentic Pasta Book*. New York: Simon and Schuster, 1985.

Plotkin, Fred. *Italy for the Gourmet Traveler*. Boston: Little, Brown, 1996.

Plotkin, Fred. *Recipes from Paradise: Life and Food on the Italian Riviera*. Boston: Little, Brown, 1997.

Plotkin, Fred. *La Terra Fortunata: The Splendid Food and Wine of Friuli-Venezia Giulia*. New York: Broadway, 2001.

Rodgers, Judy. *The Zuni Cafe Cookbook*. New York: W. W. Norton, 2002.

Rogers, Ruth, and Rose Gray. *The River Café Cookbook*. London: Ebury, 1996.

Schira, Roberta. *La Pasta Fresca e Ripiena*. Milano: Adriano Salani Editore, 2009.

Slow Food Editore. *Le forme del latte*. Bra: Slow Food Editore, 2003.

Slow Food Editore. *La Pasta*. Bra: Slow Food Editore, 2010.

Slow Food Editore. *Terra Madre 1600 comunità del cibo*. Bra: Slow Food Editore, 2006.

Talbott, Mona. *Zuppe: Soups from the Kitchen of the American Academy in Rome, the Rome Sustainable Food Project*. New York: The Little Bookroom, 2012.

Talbott, Mona and Mirella Misenti. *Biscotti*. New York: The Little Bookroom, 2010.

*The Silver Spoon*. New York: Phaidon, 2005.

Waters, Alice. *The Art of Simple Food*. New York: Clarkson Potter, 2007.

Waters, Alice, David Tanis, and Fritz Streiff. *Chez Panisse Café Cookbook*. New York: HarperCollins, 1999.

Waters, Alice. *Chez Panisse Vegetables*. New York: HarperCollinsPublishers, 1996.

Waters, Alice, Patricia Curtan, and Martine Labro. *Chez Panisse Pasta, Pizza & Calzone*. New York: Random House, 1984.

Zanini, De Vita, Oretta. *Encyclopedia of Pasta*. Berkeley: University of California, 2009.

Zanini, De Vita, Oretta., Maureen B. Fant, and Howard M. Isaacs. *The Food of Rome and Lazio: History, Folklore, and Recipes*. Rome, Italy: Alphabyte, 1994.

Websites:

cintasenese.blogspot.com/Ð

http://cmsdata.iucn.org/downloads/overview_of_the_conservation_status_of_the_marine_fishes_of_the_mediterranean_sea_rep.pdf

http://endoftheline.com/campaign/fish_facts/

http://www.montereybayaquarium.org/cr/seafoodwatch.aspx

# INDEX

# ACKNOWLEDGEMENTS

I would like to acknowledge and thank the following people for their extraordinary efforts that made this book possible.

Adele Chatfield-Taylor, AAR President and CEO, Christopher Celenza, AAR Director, the AAR Trustees, and the American Academy staff for their help and support during this process. The *dipendenti* are an infinite source of knowledge, passion, and buone forchette that have forever made a profound impact on how I cook and eat.

The Fellows, Affiliated Fellows, Fellow Travelers, Residents, and visitors at the American Academy that I have met in my six years here. To cook for such a talented community of impassioned people is a privilege that makes all the hard work worthwhile.

Angela Hederman and The Little Bookroom for her continued faith and support in the RSFP and our efforts to share the kitchen's recipes and vision.

Annie Schlechter for her amazing photography, patience, and vision. Annie's ability to capture all these difficult shots so effortlessly, to make people relax and have fun, and her flat out refusal to give in to a substandard are an inspiration to us all.

Elena Goldblatt for her tireless work ethic, thoughtfulness, and dedication not only to this project but to the RSFP as a whole. She is a true team player who has the ability to translate what I wanted to say from the get-go, and is capable of transforming it into words. How she turned my sounds and gestures into words is amazing.

Fabio Onalli and the crew from Villa Ada World Medicine for the incredible physical therapy they gave me after my accident. Their insightful knowledge and deep understanding of how to get me on my feet just 50 days after breaking my ankle allowed me to start writing this book and get back to work in only two months.

Russel Maret for his unbelievable work on the fonts of all the RSFP cookbooks, his countless trips to the various shops and stores to get equipment or supplies for us, general overall cheery disposition, and those amazing (and rather necessary) cocktails after 15-hour work days.

Laura Offeddu for all her hard work to help organize the housing and events leading up to this book, for her great work at the RSFP during my 50 days of absence, and her continued dedication to the RSFP.

Giovanni Guerrera, for just being Gio. This book never would have gotten off the ground had Elena and I not hatched a plan to keep Gio at the Academy and have him be a part of this project. I am so grateful for his amazing temperament, incredible teaching ability, patience, and kindness. It was a true honor to cook alongside Gio for two years.

Francesca Strazzullo for countless lessons and insight into Italian culture and food, and for teaching me how Italians both eat and ate. I can only hope to have passed on a tenth of what she gave to me.

My Italian family Giaccomo Colalillo, Alfredo Petti, and Veronica Salaris in Molise who always welcomed me with open arms and treated me as one of their own.

The recipe testers who took the time to give me feedback on all these recipes; it was so important to me that they translate both in Italy and America, and thanks to them, all this is a reality.

The RSFP staff, Gabriel Soare, Alessandro Lima, Tiziana Del Grosso, Tewelde Weldekidan, Tesfamichel Ghebrehawareit, and Mirella Misenti for their patience and support throughout this whole process, and their undying loyalty.

Chris Behr for dropping his whole life and coming here to become a part of our amazing team.

The 2011-2012 interns: Carlin Greenstein, Otis Kriegel, James Ehrlich, Elena Goldblatt, Joanna Hughes, Baglorius Wright III, Kevin Wieciech, Caroline Smart, Greg Mitchell, Rosalva Parada, Kyle Pierce, Alice Walton, Rachel Schleyer, Arie Peysert, Cynthia Traina, Sam Alberts, Sarah Johnson, and Matt Lorman.

Adele Chatfield-Taylor and Alice Waters, whom I thank for starting this wonderful collaboration; it has been a dream come true for me to come back to the food, culture, and country that I cherish so dearly. I hope these books help cement the foundation that was envisioned for this delicious revolution.

Mona Talbott and Alice Waters for choosing, trusting, believing in me, and being there every step of the way. It is a true honor to be their colleague and follow in their footsteps.

Above all, I would like to thank my family for convincing me that I am a cook.

—Christopher Boswell

# PASTA

## A NOTE ON THE TITLING TYPE

The Italian recipe names are set in Saturn, a typeface based on the inscription on the Temple of Saturn in the Roman Forum. The word PASTA on the cover and title page is inspired by turn of the 20th century Bolognese signage. Both were designed by Russell Maret, a type designer and letterpress printer, who was the 2010 Rolland Rome Prize Fellow in Design at the American Academy in Rome.

ABCDEFGHIJKLMNOPQRSTUVWXYZ

# AMERICAN ACADEMY IN ROME

The American Academy in Rome is a center for independent study and advanced research in the arts and humanities. For more than 116 years the Academy has offered support, time and an inspiring environment to some of America's most gifted artists and scholars. Each year, through a national juried competition, the Academy offers up to thirty Rome prize fellowships in architecture, literature, musical composition, visual arts, and in humanistic approaches to ancient studies, medieval studies, Renaissance and early modern studies, and modern Italian studies. Fellows are joined by a select group of Residents, distinguished artists and scholars invited by the Director. Many Academy Fellows and Residents have had a significant influence in the world of art, music, culture, literature, scholarship and education.

Founded in 1894, the Academy was charted as a private institution by an act of Congress in 1905. The Academy remains a private institution supported by gifts from individuals, foundations and corporations, and the membership of colleges, universities and arts and cultural organizations, as well as by grants from the National Endowment for the Humanities and the United States Department of Education.

www.aarome.org

# THE ROME SUSTAINABLE
# FOOD PROJECT

"Roma o Morte!"

In the seven years since Christopher Boswell and I launched the Rome Sustainable Food Project at the American Academy in Rome, we have often joked that making the pasta and driving the Academy's Piaggo Ape (the three-wheeled mini-truck used by the Academy's gardeners and housekeepers) are at the top of the "must do" list for nearly every RSFP intern. It is easy to understand why—pasta is the most iconic dish of the Italian food canon and the Piaggo Ape, although strictly off limits, is like a great plate of Roman pasta: simply irresistible.

Teaching cooking and pasta making on the Janiculum Hill, where the revolutionary Giuseppe Garibaldi and his Red Shirt volunteers defended Rome against the French in 1849, is a daily honor and a reminder that we are part of another revolutionary movement: the delicious revolution, begun by the visionary Alice Waters at Chez Panisse in Berkeley, California, in 1971, where both Chris and I worked and became educated in the sustainable food movement.

Chris Boswell is a passionate chef and a respected teacher. He educates and informs every intern that Italian food—not French, as commonly believed—is the fundamental cuisine to learn to cook, and that the Mediterranean diet is the ideal model for institutional dining programs. For feeding large groups of hungry workers, scholars and artists, pasta is an obvious, economical choice; and frankly it is what everyone craves.

Simple purity and astounding good taste triumph over fussy complicated interpretations, and these are the recipes that Chris and Elena have featured in *Pasta*, the third book in the Rome Sustainable Food Project's cookbook series.

Infinitely patient and employing his dry wit, Chris has taught more than one hundred young cooks to master pasta making with the clear instructions and techniques that are shown throughout the book. Chewy *pasta secca* and silky *pasta fresca* reminds us daily that well-made pasta is as serious and essential to Romans as life or death.

Mona Talbott
Brooklyn, NY

# ABOUT THE AUTHORS

Christopher Boswell is the Executive Chef of the Rome Sustainable Food Project. He has been at the RSFP since the program was established in 2006, when he was chosen by Alice Waters to work with former RSFP Executive Chef Mona Talbott.

Boswell started out as a dishwasher and a prep cook in the small gold rush town of Jackson, California. After high school, he attended the California Culinary Academy where he received the distinguished Daniel Carlisle Walker award for culinary excellence. He then went on to work at Stars, Acquarello, and One Market restaurants before moving to Italy for a year to learn authentic rustic cooking.

Chef Boswell then joined Chez Panisse, where he received five years of intensive training under Alice Waters and her brigade of distinguished chefs.

Elena Goldblatt has always had a passion for cooking. She moved to her mother's native Rome when she was 12 years old, and has been drawn back ever since. She graduated from Yale University in 2010 and was an intern in the Rome Sustainable Food Project kitchen in 2011. She worked for author and journalist Mark Bittman at *The New York Times* before returning to Rome to work with Chef Christopher Boswell on the RSFP cookbook Pasta.

# ABOUT THE PHOTOGRAPHER

Annie Schlechter is a New Yorker and has been working as a photographer since 1998. Her clients include: *New York Magazine, The World of Interiors, Veranda, Coastal Living, Travel + Leisure* and many more but she adores working on projects with *The Little Bookroom.*